LIVE. LOVE. ENGAGE.

How to Stop Doubting Yourself and Start Being Yourself

GLORIA GRACE RAND

Copyright © 2020 By Gloria Grace Rand

LIVE. LOVE. ENGAGE.

All rights reserved. No part of this publication may be reproduced, distributed, or transmitted in any form or by any means, including photocopying, recording, or other electronic or mechanical methods, without the prior written permission of the publisher, except in the case of brief quotations embodied in critical reviews and certain other noncommercial uses permitted by copyright law. For permission requests, write to the publisher, addressed "Attention: Permissions Coordinator," at info@beyondpublishing.net

"All quotes are from A Course in Miracles, copyright ©1992, 1999, 2007 by the Foundation for Inner Peace, 448 Ignacio Blvd #306 Novato, CA 94949, www.acim.org and info@acim.org, used with permission."

Quantity sales special discounts are available on quantity purchases by corporations, associations, and others. For details, contact the publisher at the address above.

Orders by U.S. trade bookstores and wholesalers. Email info@BeyondPublishing.net

The Beyond Publishing Speakers Bureau can bring authors to your live event. For more information or to book an event contact the Beyond Publishing Speakers Bureau speak@BeyondPublishing.net

The Author can be reached directly at BeyondPublishing.net

Manufactured and printed in the United States of America distributed globally by BeyondPublishing.net

BEYOND
PUBLISHING

New York | Los Angeles | London | Sydney

ISBN Hardcover: 978-1-637920-42-8

In memory of Michaela,
my cheerleader, my best friend, my sister.

I love you always.

Life is meant to be lived. You're meant to pursue your dreams, and take risks in this lifetime. This means giving your doubts a break and giving your soul a chance to speak its truth. The only thing standing in your way is you. Today, get out of your way and explore your unknown.

Gloria Grace Rand

TABLE OF CONTENTS

Introduction 7

PART I: LET GO AND LET GOD
Chapter 1: *Hiding in Plain Sight* 13
Chapter 2: *The Dreaded "C" Word* 29
Chapter 3: *Signs, Signs, Everywhere a Sign* 35

PART 2: OPEN YOUR HEART TO RECEIVE
Chapter 4: *Deflecting vs. Accepting* 51
Chapter 5: *Money, Money, Money* 55
Chapter 6: *Risks and Rewards* 59
Chapter 7: *Opening Your Heart-Mind* 65
Chapter 8: *Connecting With Your Higher Power* 73

PART 3: VALUE YOUR UNIQUENESS
Chapter 9: *Finding the Courage to Be You* 81
Chapter 10: *The Cost of Not Valuing Your Worth* 87
Chapter 11: *Synchronicities and Health Scares* 95
Chapter 12: *What's Love (and Fear) Got to Do It?* 101

PART 4: EMBRACE YOUR DIVINITY
Chapter 13: *Spiritual Soul Searching* 109
Chapter 14: *Missing The Mark* 115
Chapter 15: *Attitude of Gratitude* 121
Chapter 16: *Live Fully, Love Deeply and Engage Authentically* 129

Acknowledgements 133
About the Author 135

INTRODUCTION

Birthing this book has been the longest pregnancy I've ever experienced, and I've been blessed to carry two amazing children into this world.

The genesis for this book started in October, 2016, when my sister was two months away from transitioning from this world due to the onset of cancer the year before. After many stops and starts, partly due to the grieving process, partly due to my reluctance to place my faith totally in God's hands, the time has come for this book to finally see the light of day.

I know that in the grand scheme of things, people have taken longer to get their books written, and people have taken a shorter amount of time to write their books. Still, I am a Virgo, which means I have a perfectionist streak in me, and I also have a tendency to go whole-hog into a project and expect it to be finished in a reasonable amount of time. Ha!

As I discovered in practicing the techniques myself that I'll share in this book, patience is a virtue, and all good things come to those who wait. Also, as The Byrds' song, Turn! Turn! Turn! says, (paraphrased from the Bible):

There is a season (turn, turn, turn)
And a time to every purpose, under heaven.

Why did I finally decide to get the book done?

It took a global pandemic to light a fire under my ass!

I love the quote from Napoleon Hill, author of *Think and Grow Rich*, who said, "The time will never be just right." That's true. And yet, this is the absolute right time to get this message out into the world. In fact, I believe it's why I was brought to this planet - just for this reason - to share God's message of L.O.V.E.

You may think I sound conceited right now.

Why me? I say, why not me?

This excerpt from Marianne Williamson's poem *Our Deepest Fear* said it best:

We ask ourselves
Who am I to be brilliant, gorgeous, talented, fabulous?
Actually, who are you not to be?
You are a child of God.

Your playing small
Does not serve the world.
There's nothing enlightened about shrinking
So that other people won't feel insecure around you.

We are all meant to shine,
As children do.
We were born to make manifest
The glory of God that is within us.

8 | *Gloria Grace Rand*

Spiritually speaking - I was raised Catholic. I attended mass every week, gave up meat during Lent, but I never resonated with many of the church's teachings. And frankly, my mother didn't either. We often found ourselves making critical comments in the pew during the priest's homilies, especially when the church waded into politics.

I believed in God. I just didn't resonate with religion… at least the Catholic Church variety. I found God in nature. I felt close to God there. Nevertheless, I went through the motions of being a "good" Catholic, and attended mass every week for decades.

It was not until my sister got diagnosed with cancer that all hell (pardon the expression) broke loose for me, spiritually speaking! And thus, began the spiritual journey that birthed this book.

If you have ever had a family member or close friend go through cancer, you have my sympathy and understanding. It is not an easy job watching someone you love suffer and feeling powerless to change the outcome. You can probably relate to the mix of feelings and emotions I experienced during Michaela's 18-month cancer journey, and the grief I felt when she transitioned. I did my best to be a support system for her. I flew 2,000 miles from my home to be with her during chemotherapy treatments, but I wasn't there every time. She had to rely on her friends for support on those occasions.

It took me quite a while to get over the guilt of not being there. Thankfully, the concepts that God shared with me and that you will learn about in subsequent chapters, helped me to let go of the guilt and grief I carried. You will learn more of my story as we go along. Here's what you need to know before I continue. This book is intended to show you how to L.O.V.E. your way out of fear and self-doubt, so you can forgive the past, gain self-confidence, and create

LIVE. LOVE. ENGAGE | 9

the abundant life God intended you to have. It is divided into four parts, and at the end of each part, you'll find a variety of practices that have helped me to live fully, love deeply and engage authentically, and which I believe can help you do the same.

You've probably suspected by now that L.O.V.E. is an acronym. If so, you are right! Read on to find out what the letter "L" stands for. I'll give you a hint. It involves trust and allowing… two concepts I did not learn very well as a child! :-)

PART 1
LET GO AND LET GOD

"...with God all things are possible" Matthew 19:26

CHAPTER 1

HIDING IN PLAIN SIGHT

"Be yourself--not your idea of what you think somebody else's idea of yourself should be."

Henry David Thoreau

I once met a beautiful, spiritually-minded woman at a conference who gave me a slip of paper with two powerful questions to ask myself:

What would my life be like if I let go of the need to produce because of the need to earn money, and instead start to only focus and do and be what brings me most joy, and do only what I love?

Would that create more possibilities for me to take care of me and my dreams?

I've kept that piece of paper taped to my computer as a reminder to keep asking myself those questions. When we focus on what brings us joy, it's a lot easier to actually BE joyful. And isn't that why we're here?

I invite you to ask yourself whether focusing on doing what you love, and what brings you joy would create more possibilities for your spiritual, personal, and financial fulfillment. If that idea sounds farfetched, or you are not sure how to go about it, keep reading. This book contains a roadmap to show you how to let go of what does not serve you, to open yourself to love, and to value and appreciate who you are in this moment, so you can stop doubting yourself, and start being yourself. I believe that when that happens, you can have more peace, joy and abundance as you are able to live fully, love deeply and engage authentically.

What does it mean to "live fully" and why would you want to?

To me, living fully means living in the moment. Being truly present to the people and circumstances in your life. Putting your heart and soul into everything you do. And allowing yourself to feel the range of emotions that human beings get to express, like joy, sadness, anger, and fear.

Living fully also means to embrace life in all its wonderful messy ways. To go for it with no hesitation; to face your fears and do it anyway. To live every day as if it is your last; to have fun, make love, do your best in everything you do. To BE the best you can be and to do everything full out, 100 percent of effort.

Why would you want to live fully? Let's first look at what it means to NOT live fully. The best way to illustrate that is to show you what my life was like before I learned the lessons that will be shared in this book.

I grew up in a small, lower middle-class suburb of Detroit, Michigan, the daughter of an alcoholic father and abusive mother. I was the baby of the family. I had a brother who was 14 years older than me, and a sister, who was 10 years older. By the time I turned 8 years old,

I became an "only child" because my brother had left home to serve in the Navy, and my sister went off to college.

Dr. Bruce Lipton, author of *The Biology of Belief*, and a stem cell biologist noted for his studies of epigenetics, found that what happens during the first seven years of our life has a profound effect on our subconscious mind, which determines who we become as adults. When we experience trauma in those early years and our emotional wounds are not treated properly, the scars that develop can cause problems later in life like alcohol, gambling or food addictions, trouble keeping a job, maintaining healthy relationships, and even depression.

It's interesting that I don't have a lot of early memories. I do remember being sick frequently with the childhood illnesses of the 1960's, such as measles, chicken pox and scarlet fever. I vaguely remember being in the hospital to have my tonsils removed when I was four. Louise Hay wrote in her book, *You Can Heal Your Life*, that our mental patterns create diseases in the body. For example, the book says tonsillitis stems from fear, repressed emotions and stifled creativity. I believe my illnesses, including tonsillitis, were an unconscious attempt on my part to solicit love and attention from my family, and a response to fearful events in my life.

What was I afraid of? One memory surfaced a few years ago during an exercise I participated in while attending a personal development workshop. The exercise was intended to improve our eyesight by recalling an incident from our past that we didn't want to see. I had been wearing corrective lenses for nearsightedness since I was 6 years old, so the idea of being able to see better sounded great to me!

During the exercise, I recalled seeing a woman sleeping on the couch in our living room and feeling that she wasn't supposed to be there, since I didn't know who she was. I'm not sure how old I was when this happened, but my sense is that I was not much older than five. I suspect that my dad may have picked her up in a bar and brought her home.

My mom did tell me when I was a teenager that she wanted to divorce my dad when I was around four or five years old, but my grandmother (her mother) talked my mom out of it. (My parents eventually divorced when I was in college.) Perhaps, the woman sleeping on our couch was the trigger that ignited my mom's desire to end her marriage. It's odd that I don't remember asking my mom, point blank, why she wanted to divorce my dad. I always assumed it was his alcoholism. But maybe it was infidelity, too. Unfortunately, I can't confirm this theory since my parents and siblings are no longer alive.

Louise Hay also references nearsightedness or myopia in *You Can Heal Your Life*. The book says this condition represents fear of the future, and not trusting what is ahead. A four or five-year-old could certainly find it frightening to discover a strange woman sleeping on the couch in her home. And hearing talk of divorce could make that child fear what that event could mean for her in the future. It makes sense to me that my subconscious mind decided to protect me by causing people and things in my world to go out of focus, so I wouldn't be able to see them.

Realizing during this workshop that my nearsightedness was likely self-induced, I decided to stop wearing my contact lenses for one hour a day to determine if I could see clearly. Much to my surprise, pleasure, and the disbelief of my family, I could! My world was no longer blurry.

I gradually increased the time that my eyes were naked (without lenses), until I could go an entire day without wearing contacts. I'm now in my late 50s, and even though a lot of people my age use reading glasses or bifocals to enhance their vision, I am so grateful that I can use a computer, read a book, and drive my car without any corrective lenses. I see clearly now because I no longer fear the future.

Everything's Fine...

Fear of the future was the story of my past. Growing up with an alcoholic father, and an abusive mother caused a lot of fear and anxiety for me. There were many times when I didn't feel safe around my parents. I still remember an event that happened when I was 6 or 7 years old. My dad was taking me to ballet class and, on the way there, we stopped for dinner at Ponderosa steakhouse. After we got our food, we sat down at a table in the middle of the restaurant and began to eat our meal. I am sure I did not fully understand what being drunk was at that age. But I could tell something was wrong with him. And then the unthinkable happened. Midway through our meal, he started to heave and throw up into his plate. I was horrified and didn't know what to do. I sat there in stunned silence, and attempted to finish eating my dinner, as he pulled himself together. Thankfully, he was able to drive me to class without further incident.

My mom had a short fuse and an explosive temper. When I was little, my brother and sister bore the brunt of that anger, but I experienced my share of it too. Like the time my mom caught me scraping peas off my dinner plate into the garbage grinder because I did not like the taste of them. She whacked me so hard, I got a black eye.

That black eye eventually healed. But the yelling and screaming she heaped upon me and the rest of our family over the years took its toll on my psyche. There's an old nursery rhyme that goes, "Sticks and stones may break my bones, but words will never hurt me." That's just plain B.S. The person who wrote that never suffered from verbal abuse.

It's no wonder that I felt like I couldn't trust my parents. If you can't trust the people closest to you, who are supposed to care and protect you, how could I expect to put my trust into God?

To "let go and let God" is not a new concept. I am the first to admit that. Google that phrase and you will find over 1-1/2 billion pages of results. That is not a typo. The exact number was 1,560,000,000! The phrase essentially means to surrender your ability to solve your problem and let God do it for you. It takes a lot of guts to surrender control to a higher power, and it is one of the hardest lessons I have had to learn on my spiritual path.

Not being able to trust God, let alone others, caused me to take up a unique survival skill: hiding in plain sight. By hiding, I mean hiding my emotions. I was afraid to speak up and speak out about how I really felt because I was afraid of how it would be perceived. I was afraid of being judged. Afraid of being yelled at or hit. Instead, I strived to be perfect, to be the "good" girl. And I became hyper critical of myself and others in the process.

Not exactly a recipe for living fully. Although by outward appearances, most people probably thought I was "fine."

I excelled in school, graduating 4th in my high school class. I earned a Bachelor's Degree in Mass Communications and began working in television, serving on the staff of the Nightly Business Report, which at that time, aired on over 240 Public Broadcasting stations across the U.S. During my tenure there, I started as a character generator operator and later advanced to be a writer and producer for the show. In the meantime, I also got married, gave birth to and raised a son and daughter; I served as a Girl Scout leader, part-time substitute teacher, and today, a business owner.

All the while, I became adept at wearing a mask (not a literal mask like the one I wore during the COVID-19 pandemic), to cover my true feelings. The emotional mask I wore bore the impression of someone who was happy and satisfied with life. In fact, "Fine," had been my standard reply when anyone asked me how I was, dating back to childhood, even when I was burning up with a fever. I always felt it was safer for me to say I was fine, even when I wasn't.

The problem with this strategy is that it's exhausting pretending to be someone you're not, attempting to live up to others' expectations, striving to be perfect, and then beating yourself up when you're not. It took me many years to realize this. (I still slip up occasionally because I'm not perfect, I am human. LOL!) I said I was "fine" so much, I believed it for a very, very long time.

The cracks in my armor started to show when I was in my 40s. When my daughter was in middle school and my son in elementary school, my husband received a lucrative job offer that required us to move 200 miles away from the town where my kids had grown up. As a result, I left my job at NBR, left my role as leader of my daughter's Girl Scout troop, and left my friends behind.

Now, I had to figure out what I was going to do. There was just one problem. I didn't know who I was any more. I only knew who I wasn't. I was no longer a TV business news writer/producer. I was no longer a Girl Scout leader. I was still a wife and mother, but my kids were getting older, and before too long, would be out of the nest. In retrospect, I suppose I was having a midlife crisis!

And in times of crisis, I did what I had been doing since I was a child. I turned to food for comfort. Food never yelled at me, like my mom did. Food was always there, unlike my dad. Food made me feel good, for a short time at least. While the kids were at school, and my husband was at work, I gorged on junk food, and packed on the pounds. Eventually, I tipped the scales at nearly 200 pounds before I put the brakes on and started a healthy eating and exercise routine. But that's a story for a different book.

Let's just say, I was lonely. I was bored. I was unhappy. And nobody knew it. The lessons I learned during a college acting class must have stuck with me, because I wore that "fine" mask well.

As an example, a year after we moved, I ran the Disney World Marathon. Ok - walked is more like it. I had lost some weight by this time, but not enough that you could say I was in "peak athletic condition." It took me 7+ hours, but I crossed the damn finish line and took home my Mickey Mouse medal - raising money for the Leukemia & Lymphoma Society in the process. (That is a great program by the way. I highly recommend it if you're interested in completing a marathon, and need the training and support to do it, while supporting a worthy cause.)

Showing off my Mickey Mouse medal for completing the Walt Disney World marathon in 2006

Training for the marathon had distracted me for several months, but with the race over, I quit running. I needed a new project. Something to occupy my mind. I didn't technically need a job, since my husband made enough money to support our family. I wanted to work. I wanted something fulfilling to do. I just didn't know what that was.

I had rejected the idea of working in television again because NBR had spoiled me. Unlike local television, working in financial news meant I never had to work weekends or holidays since the stock market was closed, and we would always pre-record a show to air on those days.

After sitting around bored for a few months, I invested in a home-study course in children's writing. I imagined myself as the next J.K. Rowling, but lost interest after my stories got rejected from a couple of magazines.

In the interim, I kept receiving mail from a company called American Writers & Artists Inc. advertising a home-study copywriting course. In other words, they sent me junk mail offering to teach me how to write junk mail! I kept one of the ads on a desk shelf in my office, because something about it intrigued me. Finally, I decided to bite the bullet and invest in the program. Once I started studying the concepts and doing the exercises, I discovered I liked copywriting. As it turns out, copywriting isn't that different from business news writing. So, I decided to use my new skills and go into business for myself.

That decision turned out to be just what I needed to stretch and grow as a human being. Why? Launching a business brought up all of the fears and doubts I had about myself, as well as some limiting beliefs about money I had developed that had been buried deep in my subconscious mind since childhood.

If you're thinking that doesn't sound very appealing, you're right. It wasn't. In fact, it was downright unpleasant. But it was oh, so necessary. I had to face those fears and doubts in order to heal the trauma I suffered as a child. It's why I am now able to live fully, love deeply, and engage authentically. And as you'll start to see in the next chapter, it's how you can too.

Fear Rears its Ugly Head

I was excited about going into business, until I realized that meant I would have to become a sales person. That is the definition of business after all - it's a means of exchanging goods and services for one another or money. The problem with this concept was that I didn't like the idea of selling. I was uncomfortable talking with people I didn't know. And frankly, I was scared of being rejected. I know many small business owners feel this way. It's why they resist picking up the phone to make sales calls.

My fear of being rejected was amped up about 10x because of the trauma I experienced as a child. I was afraid to stand out and be seen, and yet there was also this deeper part of me that longed to do just that. One of the things I am grateful to my mom for was the fact that she quit smoking so she could pay for dance lessons for me. I got to express myself every year during our annual dance recital, when I performed tap, ballet, and jazz numbers with the other students.

One of the few times where I did place my faith in God happened during one of those recitals.

My dance teacher offered students the opportunity to take private lessons, so they could perform a solo routine during the recital. I had watched some of my classmates do that, and I wanted to do it too. My mom indulged me, so I started taking private lessons and performed a dance routine during the annual recital. One year, something unexpected happened during one of these performances. I stepped out onto the stage and began my tap routine just as I had rehearsed it dozens of times before. The only problem was this time, after I had executed a few steps, my mind went blank. I totally forgot the rest of the routine! Instead of freezing in place, I started to ad lib steps – a shuffle ball change here, a turn there – all the while hoping and praying that I would hear something in the music that would trigger my memory. Sure enough, that is exactly what happened. After what seemed like two minutes, but was probably more like 30 seconds, the rest of the routine kicked in and I was able to finish without incident. In fact, people complimented me on my performance when I got off the stage. No one had even noticed there was anything wrong!

I suppose you could say muscle memory was at work, or that I was acting like an experienced jazz player. I knew enough steps to keep going and that God had nothing to do with it. And you could be right. Except that I was maybe 13 or 14 years old at the time. I loved tap dancing the best. I had talent because I do not believe my teacher would have let me perform otherwise.

Yet, I still believe God had a hand in my performance. I could have easily stopped what I was doing and run off the stage in humiliation. But I did not. I know it is because I have this inner light; this God spark inside me - and you do too - that refuses to be dimmed! That is why I stuck it out, and God was right there with me, providing a calm reassurance that I would get my bearings and finish the dance as I had intended.

Performing ballet during our annual dance recital - late 1970s.

I wish I had called on God to help me with my business early on. Of course, if I had, this book might not have been written. LOL! What helped get me over my fear of sales was the fact that I realized my SEO knowledge could help others. And being in service to other people was more important to me than getting rejected.

My first big sale came about as a result of listening to a presentation by two life coaches whose topic was, "No is a complete sentence." I was impressed by them, and the next day decided to see if I could find their website on Google using the keyword phrase, "Orlando life coaches." As I scrolled through the first few pages of results, their website listing was nowhere to be found. And as I had learned in my SEO copywriting course, you want your listing to show up on Page One, because very few people continue their search beyond that first page of results.

I decided to put into practice more of what I had learned in the course by examining their website. That's when I discovered the problem that was burying their website in the search engine results pages and that it was a problem I could fix! I remember sitting in front of my computer screen, knowing I needed to contact them, but afraid of how they would react, or afraid they would think I was not qualified to help. I am not even sure what I was afraid of, I just remember being afraid. Finally, I decided, what the heck! What have I got to lose? I sent them an email in which I explained that I could not find their website on Google, but I knew why it was not visible, and more importantly, I knew what to do to correct it.

What was even more significant about this event was that I had not even finished the SEO copywriting course yet. But I knew I had learned enough to help these women out. I was confident I could get their website to show up on Google if someone were looking for a life coach. I heard back from them, and they were delighted that

LIVE. LOVE. ENGAGE. | 25

I could help because they were extremely frustrated that they had spent a lot of money on a new website that wasn't generating any new clients for them.

I wish I could say that this sale was the first of many, and within one year I was earning six-figures. I did make more sales, and it wasn't easy. I frequently struggled with how much to charge for my services. As an example, I began writing blog articles for a web designer. I wound up working for this client for 7 years. It was a steady income that I could count on each month. There was just one problem. When I first started writing for them, I agreed to be paid $40 to write a 300-word article. Even though that may not sound like a lot, I was writing about a dozen articles per month, so I was bringing in about $500-$600 in monthly revenue. That was great for the first couple of years, but as I continued to work for them, year after year, I never asked for more money. When I was a full-time employee of NBR, I had yearly reviews, and because I did well in my job, I got a modest raise every year.

In this case, I was a freelancer. I believe the company was happy to be getting great work from me for a modest cost. Every good business owner wants to keep their expenses down, so I understand why they wouldn't want to offer me more money per article. It took me about 4 years before I finally got up the nerve to ask for a $5 per article raise. And that only happened after I attended a webinar that dealt with pricing your services. Clearly, I had some issues going on here. Self-worth being chief among them. Also, some limiting beliefs about money and business that I had unconsciously picked up from my mom.

My mother had grown up during the Depression, the daughter of a coal miner in West Virginia. She didn't have much growing up, and as an adult, she always worried about money. She always felt like we didn't have enough. And she would depend on her mother to help us out financially.

The thing was - we weren't poor. We lived in a middle-class suburb of Detroit. Both of my parents worked, so our mortgage payment was always paid, and we had food to eat. Granted, it was Hamburger Helper during the recession in the 1970s, (yuck!), but it was still food. I never went to bed hungry. I did have to wear layers in the house during the winter because we kept the thermostat down to save on the heating bill, but I had clothes to wear, and we sometimes burned wood in the fireplace to keep warm too.

What I didn't have were any positive role models when it came to business. The only entrepreneur in the family was my mom's brother. But she always complained about him, calling him a crook. I don't know whether that was true or not because I never developed a close relationship with my uncle. And I couldn't seek him out for advice even if I wanted to when I started my business, because he had passed away several years earlier.

I wasn't consciously aware of my limiting money beliefs when I started my business. Beginning this new venture was scary, and exciting too. I had been an employee my entire adult life, and it was empowering to be in control of my destiny, instead of being at the mercy of an employer.

One thing I've become aware of in my life is the power of synchronicity. And how God or the Universe, if you prefer, provides help when you need it. The key is being aware - you can miss the signs if you're not watching. I'll detail more examples of how this played out in my life later. The divine intervention that helped me handle stress during the launch of my business was the introduction of meditation into my life.

As I was starting my business, the internet was picking up steam with online businesses, and somewhere along the way I came across an ad for a product from a company called Centerpointe. They had a product which promised to help you meditate eight times faster than a Zen monk, increase creativity, learning, memory, and inner peace while reducing stress, impulsiveness, and brain fog. Their CD set (now they use MP3s) featured an audio technology called Holosync®, which was placed inaudibly beneath peaceful music and environmental sounds. You could record your own affirmations and they would be played subliminally in the track.

Centerpointe's Holosync® product made a huge positive difference in my life. With regular use, the things that used to piss me off (such as bad drivers), didn't bother me as much. It raised my tolerance level a great deal. What I did not appreciate then, that I do now, was that meditation helped me connect with my higher power, which made it much easier for me to let go and let God. That practice would be needed because I was about to face a situation over which I had absolutely no control.

CHAPTER 2

THE DREADED "C" WORD

I still remember sitting on my bed talking with my sister as she described the pain she was having in her psoas muscle. I had never heard of the psoas muscle before, but she was quite familiar with it because my sister, Michaela, was a massage therapist. She told me she thought she had pulled the muscle doing some stretching after working with a client. But it had been a couple of weeks and even though she'd tried acupuncture and other modalities, the pain wasn't going away; it was getting worse. She told me she made an appointment with her general practitioner to figure out what was going on.

My sister, Michaela, pre-cancer

The next call I received from her came the dreaded news. The doctor had ordered a CT scan for my sister because he suspected ovarian cancer was the cause of her symptoms. As it turned out, that would have been the preferred diagnosis. Instead, after the ultrasound confirmed the presence of a large tumor, my sister underwent surgery to remove it. But during the operation, the surgeon discovered that the grapefruit-sized tumor was not in Michaela's ovary. It was lodged in the psoas muscle and had wrapped itself around a major artery and could not be removed without significantly risking her life. After further tests, the oncologist told my sister that she had stage four pleomorphic rhabdomyosarcoma (RMS), a type of soft tissue cancer that arises from a normal skeletal muscle cell, and typically affects children.

This diagnosis came as a shock to Michaela and to me for two reasons. Number one: we had no history of cancer in our family. Our parents died of heart disease. Number two: My sister was incredibly healthy except for this stupid tumor! The doctors couldn't explain how she contracted the disease, except to say it was so rare, it was as if she had been hit by lightning. Not very consoling, but true. RMS is so rare that there are only about 350 cases diagnosed each year in the United States in children under the age of 21. And the stats when it comes to adults are even more staggering. According to the Liddy Shriver Sarcoma Institute website, there have been five "large" published series, totaling just over 400 cases of "adult" RMS (including some "children") seen at major cancer centers in the United States and Europe over the past 20-30 years. My sister was now a member of that exclusive group, and faced radiation and chemotherapy treatments to shrink the tumor. If that was not bad enough, Michaela's oncologist said she was at "high risk of having an incomplete response to her treatment and was at high risk of having an incurable situation."

Armed with this news, I immediately went into fix-it mode. I couldn't bear the thought of losing my sister. Not only was Michaela the last surviving member of the immediate family I grew up with, but she was also my best friend and my cheerleader. She was the one I could turn to when I had a bad day in my business or in my marriage. She would lend a sympathetic ear, listen to me vent, and remind me that I was doing well. And I was happy to play that role for Michaela as well, listening to her describe what was going on in her massage business and in her personal life.

I started searching online, as one does when confronted with a health problem, to find a solution including alternative treatments that could give her a better prognosis. At one point, I suggested that she go to Mexico because some patients had seen promising results there. But Michaela wasn't interested. She felt it would be too expensive, and she was nervous about having enough money to live on. As a self-employed massage therapist, who could no longer work because of the cancer, Michaela had to tap into her savings to pay for living expenses like her mortgage payment, food, and utilities.

I tried to persuade Michaela that my husband and I could help her out financially, but she would not go for it. She preferred to follow conventional treatment, especially since after she paid her deductible, everything else – the cost of radiation, chemotherapy and pain medication - was covered 100 percent under her health insurance plan.

The tumor had made it too painful for my sister to walk, so she had to use a wheelchair to get around. After Michaela started chemotherapy, she was too sick to work anyway. If you've been around anyone who has gone through chemo, you know that it not only kills the cancer cells, it kills the healthy cells in your body too, leaving you weak and nauseous, and at high-risk of infection.

The other challenge for my sister was that she was divorced, with no kids. All she had for support were her friends, work colleagues and me. And I lived 2,000 miles away! Michaela had always prided herself on being an independent woman. Cancer kicked that idea in the butt.

Now, my big sister had to let go and let God into her life, by asking people to take her to doctors' appointments and chemotherapy treatments, to cook meals for her, and make sure she was taking her medications properly. That meant allowing her friends, co-workers, and me to see her when she was far from her best. My sister was now forced to be vulnerable, to let her guard down, and that wasn't easy for her. On the other hand, being vulnerable meant she could engage authentically with those around her. Grudgingly at first, she started to let people know how she felt, and what she needed help with. Sometimes, those closest to her didn't want to know how she felt because, if you've ever been in constant pain, or been around someone who has, you've probably seen how it can affect your emotions – making you short-tempered and dare I say, downright bitchy! My dear sister would lash out from time to time. And as a result, I would get phone calls from her friends, asking how soon I could be back in Arizona to take care of her. They had their own families, and even though they loved my sister, they didn't like getting yelled at. Nobody does, right?

I know Michaela didn't want to hurt anybody's feelings. But it was frustrating for her to be in pain and to be so vulnerable. I can still hear her exasperated voice saying, "God, did you have to give me cancer to teach me how to ask for help?"

The answer was, "Yes!" Asking for help was a lesson I had to learn too.

Me and Michaela, Thanksgiving, 2015

CHAPTER 3

SIGNS, SIGNS, EVERYWHERE A SIGN

Trusting my intuition was not something I excelled at before my sister got sick. Quite the contrary. I can't even begin to count the number of times in my life when I had a gut feeling or heard a voice in my head say, "go this way," or "do that thing," only to disregard it, and then regret it later. Most of the time, ignoring my intuition meant minor inconveniences, like getting caught at a red light, or stuck in traffic. But there were other times when I got burned by it, and wound up in a minor fender bender, for example. Or I would say, "Yes" when someone asked me to do something, even though I my gut was telling me not to do it. And then, I would just feel miserable and taken advantage of, when it was my own fault for not sticking up for myself and trusting my intuition.

Thankfully, I started letting go of the need to control events and started to let God play a more direct role in my life. As a result, my life has been transformed for the better. It all started with what I now call my "divine download."

I can remember the day like it was yesterday. It was Tuesday, October 25, 2016 - the day after the Unconference - a multi-day event I had attended in Orlando, FL that was hosted by the Women's Prosperity Network. I have been a member of WPN for several years and had joined the group to meet other women and to learn and grow my SEO copywriting business.

That morning, I got up and took our two dogs out for a walk, and came back to my office to meditate, as I would usually do. However, this meditation session was like no other I had experienced before. As I sat quietly in my office, I heard a voice in my head say, "You need to write a book about love." My immediate reaction was, "WHAT???? Where did that idea come from? What do I know about love? I write about online marketing." Which I did. I had a blog and wrote articles about search engine optimization, copywriting, and social media marketing to promote my business and demonstrate my expertise as an SEO Copywriter - the furthest thing away from love that I could imagine.

Looking back at that event now, I can only laugh at my insecurity, or lack of faith, I guess is a better way to describe it. Of course, I knew a thing or two about love. For heaven's sake, I loved my sister. I was spending time with her every chance I could - flying from my home in Florida to hers in Arizona to help out while she went through the chemo treatments. I was a wife and mother of two wonderful children (still am, by the way!). I loved them, and cared for them, as I had loved my parents and brother too. The reason I felt the way I did at the time was because I was under the misguided belief that to write a book about love, you needed to be an "expert" at it. To my mind, an "expert" on love was one who has studied the subject, who is a therapist, or psychologist or academic researcher. Not someone like me, a former television business news writer/producer, turned SEO copywriter.

Nevertheless, for some reason, I let go of my doubt, sat down at my computer, and started writing about this idea. As I started to type, more ideas poured out of me. Much to my surprise, love turned out to be an acronym. I received further confirmation that God was serious about my writing a book later that day, while scrolling through my email. My eyes nearly bugged out at one message. It was from Hay House - the publisher of books by such legendary personal development and spiritual authors as Dr. Wayne Dyer, Louise Hay, Christiane Northrup, and Gregg Braden. The email was offering a Writers' Bootcamp, where they would teach you how to write a book! I remember looking up at the ceiling of my office, and saying out loud, "Well... I guess you're serious about me writing a book about love, huh, God?"

I immediately invested in the course... but writing the book would have to wait. That is because while I was at the Unconference, my sister had developed a bowel obstruction, a frequent complication for patients with advanced cancer. Three days after my divine download, I got a call from one of my sister's friends who said Michaela had been admitted to the hospital because she was not doing well at all. A short time later, I got a call from a nurse at the hospital, urging me to fly out there immediately, which I did. God bless Southwest Airlines, because not only did they get me on an afternoon flight that day, but they gave me TSA pre-approval, so I was able to skip the long security line and get on the plane right away. That was so appreciated because I was a nervous wreck, praying all the way that she would live long enough for me to see her again.

Thankfully, Michaela pulled through that immediate crisis. But the only thing the hospital could offer her was palliative radiation treatment to ease the pain, and my sister said no. She decided, if it's not going to cure, what's the point? We both agreed that hospice care would be the best option for her now.

Trusting God's Plan

As I have said before, I believe the Universe conspires in our favor. Not only that, but I also believe that if we pay attention to the signs, God, Source, the Universe, whatever you want to call it, leads us to the path where we can have the most growth, which will allow us to live fully, love deeply and engage authentically.

Looking back on my life, I see patterns where one road led to another road, which led me to where I am today. For example, I majored in **business** administration in college before switching to mass communications with an emphasis on Radio/TV/Film. I found a job in television, working for the Nightly **Business** Report. And for the last ten years, I've owned and operated my own **business**. See the connection?

Those weren't obvious signs to me at the time. For instance, my first two years in college as a business major were awful. That may surprise you since I had graduated near the top of my high school class. However, the reason is because my brother, Eric, died unexpectedly in the middle of my freshman year. It was Mother's Day, and my mom was royally pissed that the day had passed without my brother calling, let alone stopping by, to wish her a happy Mother's Day. After we finished eating dinner, she called his house to cuss him out. His roommate answered the phone, went to check on him, and found Rick lying in his bed, unresponsive. My brother had died in his sleep at the young age of 33.

The rest of that spring and summer was a blur, as our family dealt with the fallout from Rick's death. When fall came, and it was time to start my sophomore year at college, I was a mess. Academically speaking, I didn't fare any better than in my freshman year. Frankly, things were getting worse.

I wound up on academic probation. I tried to hide the university's letter notifying me about that fact from my mom, but she found out. After initially losing her temper over it, she calmed down and we talked. She realized I was suffering from Rick's death too. We decided I should see my guidance counselor for help. The counselor had me take an aptitude test, and the results showed that an ideal major for me would be Mass Communications. Just one problem. I was living at home, driving to classes at the University of Michigan-Dearborn campus. But that campus did not offer that major. I would have to transfer to U of M's main campus in Ann Arbor, and live in a dorm. I did not want to leave my mom, who was grieving my brother's death. I got into Wayne State University in Detroit instead, which was a half-hour drive from our house, and that is where I got my bachelor's degree.

I started getting an inkling of God's plan for me when I recalled how I got a job working for the Nightly Business Report. A friend of mine told me she had seen a classified ad in the Miami Herald for a receptionist job at the local public television station, WPBT. I figured it wouldn't hurt to apply for that type of job, since it would be a good way to get my foot in the door. But when I looked in the paper, I saw another ad from WPBT that sounded more interesting – and in line with my communications degree. It was for a position called Electronic News Systems Operator. The job entailed helping the newsroom personnel use their new computer system and operate the character generator to produce graphics for the show. I went in for an interview, and after the person they initially offered the job to turned them down, they offered it to me – which I promptly accepted! I used to find it ironic that someone who flunked out of economics and changed her major from business administration wound up working for a business news show. Now, I know it was serendipitous.

LIVE. LOVE. ENGAGE | 39

I became more aware of God's intervention in my life after my sister's cancer diagnosis. At the time, I was working with a coach, who suggested that I launch a mastermind since it would be a great way for me help a group of people and make more money as a result. Shortly thereafter, I received an email from a coach named Jay Fiset who was leading a course on how to run masterminds. I thought, hmm, this is divine intervention, and I signed up for it. That mastermind bootcamp led me to join Jay's LEAD mastermind program, where I learned how to facilitate masterminds and workshops, and where I met the most amazing people who supported me after my sister's passing.

Another example of serendipity came a few weeks after my sister's transition. I had sold her house, and gotten rid of furniture, knickknacks, etc. She had quite a few books that I sold or donated to the local library. But I kept a few that looked interesting, by authors like Deepak Chopra and Eckhart Tolle. One afternoon, I started going through some of her old books and was stunned by a title that leaped out at me. The book was called, *Grieving Mindfully - A Compassionate and Spiritual Guide to Coping with Loss* by Sameet Kumar. Talk about a message from God and my sister! (I highly recommend that book for anyone who is grieving.)

What these examples have in common is that I let go of "how" I was going to run a mastermind, write a book about love, or even deal with the grieving process, and I let God provide the answers!

This is not a new idea. Author Mike Dooley frequently talks about the cursed "hows" and that the path to success occurs when we choose not to worry about the "hows" and leave it up to the Universe to provide the answers.

Here is a fun example of how letting go and letting God made a positive difference in my life:

One morning, as I was on the beach writing the first draft of this book, (and before our lives got disrupted by COVID-19), about a dozen young men and women lifeguards showed up and started playing soccer about 10-15 feet in front of me. They were close enough that I thought I could easily get hit by the ball if it got kicked the wrong way!

I decided to move my chair closer to the water because I was afraid that they would crash into me. I started getting quite irritated, because it seemed that no matter how far I moved my chair away from them, they kept coming closer to me. So, I stopped writing, closed my journal, and pondered, why was I getting so upset?

I decided it didn't matter. I would relax and trust that I'd be able to write my book in peace. As soon as I did that, they ended their game and left the beach! That's letting go and letting God take care of me in a nutshell.

That example may lead you to believe that the concept of "Let Go and Let God" is easy. It is a simple choice you can make. That doesn't mean it's easy. For me, it's been a lesson I've had to keep learning and applying over and over again. Just when I think I've got it; more stuff has come up from my past that I've had to release.

One of the lessons I had to learn was how to let go of the need to control everything and put God in charge. I thought I could save money in my business by doing all the tasks myself, like marketing, sales, and bookkeeping. But not hiring help for my business meant I often worked weekends. I would forget to follow up with sales leads because I was too busy scheduling social media posts. And my podcast was not growing as fast as I would have liked because I was the one doing all the editing, creating graphics, scheduling interviews, and posting graphics on social media sites.

Once I decided to let go of my need to manage everything myself, and let God handle the "how" of getting the work done, opportunities came my way. For instance, one of my clients, who was an accountant, told me that the county I lived in was offering COVID-19 grants for business owners. He suggested we barter services. I wrote some emails for him, and he helped me apply for the grant, which I then received! Once the money came in, I looked for a podcast editor. The first person I interviewed, sounded great, but her services were expensive. Then I remembered that Fiverr could be a good resource. I searched that website, and found a brilliant editor who could do the same work for a lot less money. Suddenly, I could breathe again, as a heavy load had been lifted from my shoulders. It was such a relief to delegate that work to someone else, who did a better job editing and writing show notes than I did! That's what I call a win-win.

I have also had to let go of that Big Kahuna limiting belief that so many of us share: the "I'm not worthy" story. That has been the biggest challenge of them all for me. One weekend, I decided to get away by myself to work on the book, so I got a hotel room near the beach, and spent the morning at the ocean to get inspired. On the way back to the hotel to write, I stopped off at a grocery store to get a sandwich for lunch and bought a package of cookies or chips (I do not remember which). After eating the sandwich, I proceeded to binge out on the junk food. As I was eating, I started thinking about why I was sabotaging myself in this way. I started asking myself, what was I afraid of? I began journaling and what I began to remember were all the times when I was incredibly young when I did something "bad." Here are a few examples:

I wrote on the living room wall in crayon. I have a vague memory of shoplifting something when I was probably 3 or 4 years old, but my mom (or dad) caught me before we left the store. I played with matches once and almost set the rug in our family room on fire. I sat at someone else's desk in first grade that was closer to the chalkboard because I couldn't see very well, and I remember getting in trouble because I had torn up papers in that child's desk.

What I realized as these memories flooded back into my brain was that these were the signs of a small child acting out to get attention. I had seen my brother and sister get yelled at from my mom when they did something she judged as being wrong. Yelling may have been negative attention, but it was attention nonetheless. After I got that black eye for throwing away peas, I moved to the other extreme and strived to be the "good" girl.

The problem here was that even as I excelled at school, I did not get the positive attention I craved from my mom or dad. I wanted approval, recognition that my hard work was paying off. But instead, I got yelled at for any infraction, like staying out a few minutes past curfew or not keeping my bedroom clean. Getting all A's was expected. I didn't get any special praise for it, which is what I wanted so desperately.

I realized in that moment that my bouts of sabotage, such as gaining weight after spending months dieting, or not taking action in my business to make it as successful as it could be, were all about seeking attention. If getting thin or landing a new client didn't win accolades from those closest to me, I'd sabotage myself in order to attract negative attention. It was a lose-lose proposition because I was seeking outside validation.

If you don't read and apply any more of this book than what you'll read in the next paragraph, I will feel as if I've done my job. (Please keep reading, however. There is more good stuff ahead, I promise!)

As Rick Nelson famously sang in his hit record, *Garden Party*, "You see, ya can't please everyone, so **ya got to please yourself.**"

I've been a people pleaser all of my life. Even before that afternoon's revelation, I'd been coming to terms with that. But it wasn't until that day, that I truly understood the depths of WHY I was a people pleaser. And why I now had to start pleasing myself first. That's the only way I could be happy, and it's the only way you can too.

I know many people think it's selfish to put yourself first. Tough. Even flight attendants instruct you to put the air mask on yourself first before helping family members. They know if you can't breathe, you die, and then you won't be able to help those who can't help themselves. It's as simple as that.

That afternoon, I let go of the pain. I let go of the shame. I let go of the grief over so much time wasted. And I let go of the need to beat myself up for NOT being perfect! And when the tears had subsided, a feeling of calm and peace washed over me.

Letting go and letting God into my life has been instrumental to my healing process. And I am also not going to lie to you and say that all you need to do is read this book, and you will be happy, healthy, wealthy, and wise. It is not up to me anyway. You have the power to decide how you want to be, and how you want to feel in any given moment. Tony Robbins says you can change your state with a snap of your fingers. The Latin origin of the word "decide" means to "cut off." When you decide, you cut off all other possibilities to focus on a particular direction. So, you can decide to live fully, love deeply, and engage authentically and just do it!

You think, "Easy for you to say…" I hear you because I have been there. This is where letting go and letting God comes into the picture. Trusting in God really means trusting in yourself. It means acknowledging that you have a spiritual nature, and when you raise your vibration to focus on the good in your life, more good will come. Ask first, then trust in God to deliver.

I believe the L.O.V.E. Method in this book and the practices at the end of this chapter will aid you in your spiritual journey, as will other spiritual and personal development books that I have read and benefited from including *The Power of Now* by Eckhart Tolle, *Erroneous Zones* by Wayne Dyer, *The Vortex* by Esther and Jerry Hicks, and *Radical Forgiveness* by Colin Tipping.

You may also consider studying *A Course in Miracles*. The lessons in this course made a tremendous difference in my relationship to God, and were instrumental in my transformation. Marianne Williamson's book *Return to Love* and *A Course in Miracles Made Easy* by Alan Cohen are excellent resources to facilitate your understanding of the course.

Getting support in a group setting by attending a personal development workshop is useful too. I personally recommend The Gift and The Launch that are conducted by The Creators Code. Working one-on-one with a coach, therapist, minister, or counselor can also be highly beneficial too.

L.O.V.E. PRACTICES

Whoever lives in love lives in God, and God in them. There is no fear in love. But perfect love drives out fear, because fear has to do with punishment. The one who fears is not made perfect in love. ~ 1 John 4:16-18

I believe the following practices can help you to Let Go and Let God when you find yourself in times of stress or confusion about what to do, or when you've suffered some type of loss – such as a death, divorce, or even losing a job. My advice is to try one or all of them - not necessarily at the same time - and see what works best for you.

Breathe

When you are under stress, feeling down, take a few moments to take a few deep breaths. Inhale, hold it for 3 seconds, and exhale. Repeat that 2 or 3 times. You'll find that your body immediately relaxes and your mind relaxes too.

Meditate

Spend as little as 2 minutes, or as long as you like, sitting with your eyes closed. Focus on your breath, and let any thoughts in your head go. Silently acknowledge them, and refocus your attention to your breath.

There are many varieties of meditation you can try, including guided meditation, mindful meditation, Vipassana meditation, just to name a few. If you've never meditated before, the easiest way to start is to just sit quietly and focus on your breath. You can repeat a mantra, or phrase in your head silently too. I have said things like "Maranatha" which means, "Lord, come." Sanskrit words like Om or Ram are useful as well. Or I've repeated, "I am peace" over and over again to help calm myself down. Experiment to find out what works best for you.

Prayer

If you are a member of any of the major religions in the world, you likely pray already. If prayer makes you feel good, then go for it! I'm not here to tell you what to believe or how to practice it. I can only share what I've come to believe - which is that we are all spiritual beings having a human experience. I believe we are all connected and letting go and letting God into our lives is the first step in being able to love ourselves completely, so we are then able to love one another too.

Affirmations

When you are feeling stressed or unsure, repeating affirmative phrases to yourself can help you release what is bothering you so you can reconnect with your Inner Being. One of my favorite affirmations is one that Louise Hay shared:

"Out of this situation only good will come. This is easily resolved for the highest good of all concerned. All is well and I am safe."

Of course, you can also come up with your own affirmations. Here are some other common ones which may prove useful to you: I am safe. I am worthy. I am love. I am joy. I am peace.

You may notice that I am using the "I AM" statement in creating the affirmations. That is because the words, I AM are the most powerful words in the Universe. The words are the name of God. In the Bible, when Moses asked God to reveal his name, God said, "I AM WHO I AM."

Since you are a part of God, these words represent the divine in you. When you declare "I am ..." you are acknowledging that this is the truth of your being. And it will be the most powerful affirmation you can say.

PART 2

OPEN YOUR HEART TO RECEIVE

"When you open your heart with a quiet mind love rushes in."
— Genevieve Gerard

CHAPTER 4

DEFLECTING VS ACCEPTING

The second pillar in the L.O.V.E. Method is Open Your Heart to Receive.

I can hear your mind whirring with a question right now… receive what?

Ah… that's the $64,000 question, isn't it?

The answer didn't come to me right away. I think God intended it on purpose because I was supposed to figure it out on my own. It reminds me of the scene at the end of the Wizard of Oz when Glinda the Good Witch told Dorothy that she always had the power to go back to Kansas, she only had to learn it for herself.

Let's start with the idea of "receiving" in general.

I don't know how it is in other cultures, but here in the United States in my experience, boys are encouraged to stick up for themselves, and even fight for what they want. But girls are taught that we should be modest, demure, and we shouldn't ask for what we want because that would seem selfish. At least, this is it how it was when I was growing up in the 1960s. I believe things are slowly changing - at least, I hope so!

LIVE. LOVE. ENGAGE | 51

For instance, many women deflect or shrug off compliments, instead of accepting them graciously. There's this feeling that if we were to accept the kudos, we'd be bragging. Professional women often downplay their skills. They respond to compliments from colleagues or clients with comments like, "It's no big deal," or "It was nothing," or "So-and-So did all the work."

When you respond in this way, you're diminishing yourself and your efforts. Many business owners who deflect compliments also find it hard to charge for what they're worth. Can you see why? They don't value themselves. And as a result, they're always chasing clients, instead of having clients come to them.

This was a lesson I had to learn the hard way. It's why I labored for years to make a decent profit in my business. I didn't place a high enough value on my skills as a copywriter and marketer. I had also grown up believing that it's better to be modest; bragging about yourself is wrong; and people don't like people who boast about themselves.

But when you're in business, you have to let people know you're good at what you do. There's no point in being the best kept secret in town. Those companies go out of business. People need to know that you do good work. So, when a client pays you a compliment, accept it. Say, "thank you." And get them to put that testimonial in writing or say it in a video!

Opening your heart to receive compliments serves an important purpose. It demonstrates that you value the person giving the compliment. That person is being generous in telling you how much your action, your product, your service, and dare I say it, how much YOU meant to them. When you shrug it off, you are dishonoring them. You're belittling them. And if you do that enough, you're going to stop receiving compliments altogether and then, where will you be? Broke and lonely is a definite possibility. I believe with all my heart that God doesn't want that for you. God wants you to be, do, and have all that you desire. That means being open to receive compliments in whatever form they arrive.

Besides, God has given you certain gifts. And if you're not valuing those gifts by deflecting compliments about them, you're devaluing God too. You're saying God doesn't matter. You're telling the Universe that the gifts don't matter. And if they don't matter to you, how are they going to matter to your clients?

This is all a reflection of the ego talking. That voice inside our heads that thinks it's protecting us, but it's only keeping us small and dimming our light. Think about it. How can the ego protect you when it's telling you, "You don't matter, your gifts don't matter, and God doesn't matter?" That sounds like an enemy, not a friend and protector. Even Dr. Wayne Dyer used to say, ego stands for "Edging God Out."

Here is one of the important lessons to learn. You have a choice. It's within your control. You can choose to listen to the ego. Or you can choose to listen to your higher power. I guarantee you that the message you'll get from God is one of support, not criticism. How can I guarantee? Because I have faith. A friend once told me, "even if you don't believe in God or a higher power, God believes in YOU!" I agree. Let that statement empower you and embolden you to receive all the compliments and gifts that God has given you.

Mastering the ability to receive a compliment graciously can help enhance your self-esteem. The challenge for many people is learning how to accept money graciously. That issue proved problematic for my sister when one of her clients gave her a big holiday bonus.

CHAPTER 5

MONEY, MONEY, MONEY

A year or two before Michaela's cancer diagnosis, she called to tell me that one of her massage therapy clients had given her a $1000 holiday bonus, and she wanted my opinion about whether to accept it or not. Michaela felt it was too much money, and the idea of receiving this gift made her feel uncomfortable.

I, on the other hand, thought it was marvelous that one of her clients felt so highly about her that she would give such a generous gift. Rather than just tell her to accept the money without another thought, I asked Michaela how long she had been treating this client. She replied, "A couple of years."

I asked, "Has she gotten relief from you?"

Michaela answered, "Oh, yes."

In fact, my sister told me that her client, Beth, had been to several massage therapists but had not enjoyed lasting pain relief until Michaela started working with her.

Michaela went on to say that Beth had also referred other people to her for massage therapy. I told Michaela, "If the client is happy and wants to give you the money, it would be rude to refuse it." I went on to explain that the bonus was the client's way of showing how much she appreciated all the pain relief she had received as a result of Michaela's healing hands. That relief was truly priceless. I also told her that if she were to reject the gift, her client might be offended because it would seem as if my sister was rejecting her.

In the end, Michaela told me she would accept the bonus graciously and gratefully. However, Michaela told me she was not going to spend the money. Instead, she tucked it away in a drawer for a "rainy day." Michaela's willingness to open her heart to receive her client's gift proved to be the right decision since that money was used to pay bills when the cancer made it impossible for my sister to work any longer.

Why did my sister feel she couldn't accept that holiday bonus? She was an accomplished massage therapist, with loyal clients who referred her to their friends and colleagues. Even though Michaela didn't come right out and tell me why, I suspect it's because she didn't feel she deserved it. And that's because deep down in her subconscious mind, she felt unworthy.

This is a common belief that nearly every human being has at one time or another. It happens the first time we get told, "No" by a parent or other family member. That "no" is usually intended to protect us from getting hurt. Our immature brains and emotions don't necessarily see it that way. As babies, we were used to instant gratification. We cried, and someone would feed us or change our diaper. As we moved from crawling to walking, parents worried that when we fell, we'd get hurt. I felt that way with my kids! It's natural.

Parents (the vast majority of them anyway) want to protect their children. They want to keep us safe. So, when we're told, "No," it's also natural for us to ask, why? Because our brains are still forming, we don't have the intellectual capacity and reasoning to understand why we're told no. Instead, we feel disappointed and hurt by the rejection. And the problem gets compounded when parents or teachers or other significant people in your life say things like, "you're stupid" or "you're fat" or "you're a bad boy or bad girl." There is a part of you that believes it.

There is a fundamental reason why most parents want to protect their children. They do it out of love. That's the missing word I spoke about at the beginning of the chapter. It is vital for human beings to open our hearts to receive love, even if it is risky to do so.

CHAPTER 6

RISKS AND REWARDS

Love comes in many different shapes and sizes. It is the holiday bonus my sister received from her client. It is the compliment you receive from a client, friend or loved one. It's a simple act of kindness - like putting the toilet seat down when you're finished using it. (I am overjoyed when my husband does this!)

The problem I had with opening my heart to receive love in the form of an act of kindness, or assistance in my personal life or business was that I did not know how to ask for help!

Most of the time I was too scared to ask for what I wanted. Plain and simple. I was afraid that my mom would say no, or worse, yell at me. I think that is why my dad did not talk much in our house. I suspect he did not want to get in an argument with my mom either. So, I wound up modeling his behavior.

I also modeled my mother's behavior when it came to her unwillingness to pay people for help. On one hand, I admired her tenacity and determination to be self-reliant. On the other hand, her reliance on me for cheap labor when I was a teenager, proved costly. At the time, my dad was using a motorized scooter to get around because his legs had been amputated due to hardening of the arteries from smoking and alcohol abuse. That meant the jobs he used to do around the house, like yardwork, had to be done by me. There was one project that I could not do alone, and that was removing the window air conditioner from our living room in the fall to put storm windows up to keep out the winter chill. Since my mom would not pay for a handyman to do the job, the two of us had to push that HEAVY A/C unit into the house. Her frugal "we can do it ourselves" attitude caused my back to go out, a painful situation that continues to plague me off and on to this day. It has been so bad at times that I can't even stand up straight, and as a result, I have lost time at work, and spent a ton of money on chiropractor treatments to get my spine back in alignment.

You would think I would have learned a lesson from that experience. But no. For years, I was reluctant to ask for help because I decided it was easier to deal with problems myself. For instance, I would tell my husband I would do the dishes, even though he was willing to do them for me. When I broke my ankle and had my leg in a cast, I stood on one leg at the stove cooking dinner because I did not want to ask for help!

In essence, I was playing the dual roles of victim and martyr. Since I refused to ask for help, I wound up putting the needs of others before my own, which then made me feel angry and resentful. The thought process in my mind was, "Why don't they know what I need? Why do I have to tell them? Can't they see for themselves?"

Going into business for myself helped me see that I could not keep playing the martyr role. I needed to be a leader. But it took me a few years to embrace that concept. At the beginning, I fell into the trap that many entrepreneurs fall into when starting a business. You feel that you must do everything yourself. Many times, it is because you simply cannot afford to hire anyone when you are starting out. But also, you may feel that your business is your baby, and no one can run it like you can!

The problem with trying to wear the many hats a business owner must wear - such as sales manager, marketing exec, accountant, customer service rep - is that there are only so many hours in the day to do these jobs! And if you want to have a life outside of your business for family and friends, it is just not sustainable. You must get help.

That help can come in many different forms. It can be hiring a coach, hiring a virtual assistant, joining a mastermind or coaching group. The point is that there comes a time when you either burn out or you ask for help and open your heart to receive it. Sometimes, it takes reading a good book (like this one, I hope!).

Love... hurts

Opening your heart to receive love doesn't come without risk however. You can be accepted, or you can be rejected, criticized, and even ridiculed. When this happens at an early age, it can create or reinforce the belief that you're not worthy to be loved.

One of my most vivid memories of opening my heart only to get it stomped on came during second grade. For a few days in a row, I chased a boy named Timothy around the playground at lunchtime because I wanted to kiss him. One day during Show and Tell, Timothy stood up and told the class and our teacher what I was doing. The room erupted in laughter, and I felt my cheeks burn with shame and embarrassment because their reaction reinforced my belief that I wasn't worthy of affection.

In that moment, I made an unconscious decision that it was painful to show someone you care, so it's better to keep those feelings to yourself. That decision cost me dearly as I grew into adulthood. Hiding my feelings kept me from receiving the love I so desperately wanted because I was too scared to let people know how I really felt about them, so I wore the "fine" mask and pretended everything was ok. Wearing that mask meant that I was not able to engage authentically with my classmates in school. I only had a few close girlfriends, and only one best friend that I would dare let see who I was behind the curtain, and what life was like living with an alcoholic parent.

When it came to the opposite sex, let's just say, I conveyed a vibe that did not interest boys. As a result, I did not date in high school, and no one asked me to the prom. But I did not let that stop me from going, because I was not going to miss out on the penultimate high school experience! I took matters into my own hands. I asked a friend who had graduated two years earlier, and he graciously accompanied me to the dance. Turns out, the dance was not all it was cracked up to be, but no regrets. I had a gorgeous dress complete with hoop skirt, (the fashion in 1980), and I looked and felt fabulous!

As I recalled this memory about the prom, it occurred to me that even though for most of my life, I did not like asking for what I wanted, there were exceptions to the rule. When a situation was important enough to me, I did have the courage to speak up. The prom was one of those rare occasions when I stepped out of my comfort zone and asked for what I wanted.

One of the important things about growing up is it gives us a chance to start flexing our independence muscles. We start to break away from our parents and test our limits. This can be painful, but if we have support from the adults in our lives, we can truly stretch our wings and begin to fly.

For all my mom's faults, I must give her credit where credit is due, and that is when I was about to graduate from college; she gave me the best graduation gift. No, it wasn't a car.

She let me move to Florida without her.

The two of us had been dreaming of a life in Florida ever since my grandmother moved there 14 years earlier. We had been spending every Christmas vacation in Coral Gables, and let me tell you, sunshine, warm weather, and palm trees were a wonderful change of pace from snowy, cold Michigan!

My mom soon planned to retire from her job as a Wayne County Juvenile Court Officer in Detroit and relocate to Florida, away from the snow and ice. But she did not want me to wait another year for that to happen. One night, we were sitting in a movie theater waiting for the show to start, when she turned to me and said, "Glor, I'm divorcing you. You should move to Florida right after graduation."

I was shocked to say the least and delighted. Since I was graduating in December, we decided that our annual Christmas trip would be the perfect opportunity for me to pack up my stuff and make the move. I rented a cheap little duplex apartment, two doors down from my Grandmother's apartment. I was still close to family, but I was on my own -- FREEDOM!!!!

My mom modeled how to let go of her emotional and physical attachment to me. But I still had more work to do when it came to letting go of the pain and the trauma I experienced growing up. That "Show and Tell" childhood memory I talked about earlier stayed with me all these years because our brains are hardwired to register negative events more readily than positive events. Psychologists call it negativity bias. As a result, we remember insults more than praise, and traumatic experiences more than joyful experiences.

Even though our brains have a "negativity bias," we also have the power to counteract it. Scientists have found that the brain can reorganize itself by forming new neural connections throughout life. This ability is called neuroplasticity. As author Norman Doidge, MD writes in his book, "*The Brain That Changes Itself*," researchers have performed many experiments that demonstrate how we can replace bad behaviors with better ones, or even learn a new skill like playing the piano through mental practice that strengthens neuronal connections and creates new ones.

I did not know about neuroplasticity when I started my business. I did not even know about business when I started my business! If you'll recall, I changed my major in college from business administration to mass communications. Since I never learned anything about marketing, sales, or accounting in school, I had to pick these skills up as I went along. And since I was reluctant to ask for help, I struggled way longer than I needed to. Once I was able to face the limiting beliefs I had created about myself, my healing process truly began in earnest.

The book that started me on my spiritual journey was Eckart Tolle's *The Power of Now*. I can't remember when I read it originally; it may have been the year before I started my business. Even though it didn't have a direct effect on my life at that time, the seeds were planted. And that's all it takes to start shifting how we think about things, so we will be able to open our hearts to receive love.

CHAPTER 7

OPENING YOUR HEART-MIND

As much as God wanted me to learn how to open my heart to receive love in any of its different forms, I also had to learn how to open my heart to receive new ideas. I can hear your brains buzzing right now. "Wait!!! New ideas are the brain's area. It controls our senses which allow us to see, hear and touch what's going on in our surroundings." Yes... and the heart plays a role too. You've likely heard or even said something like this in the past, "I've had a change of heart." Which really means, you changed your mind! Another expression you may have used when you know something to be true is, "you know it in your heart of hearts."

And of course, there's the expression, "follow your heart," which to many people means you're acting in response to how you feel - or as Mr. Spock would say, "You're being most illogical." But Captain Kirk or Dr. McCoy would likely disagree, and so would I. Following your heart means following your intuition, which also means following your Higher Self.

Even if you don't believe in God or a "Higher Self," scientists are now aware that the heart has its own "little brain" which communicates with the brain in our head, as well as other organs of the body. J. Andrew Armour, MD, PhD, of the University of Montreal led a team of scientists studying the relationship between the heart and the brain and found that the heart contains about 40,000 specialized neurons, or sensory neurites, which form a communication network within the heart, similar to what is found in the brain.

Gregg Braden, best-selling author and a pioneer in bridging science with spirituality, has said that the heart's brain converts emotions into the electrical language of the nervous system so that its messages make sense to the brain.

What does this have to do with opening your heart to receive? It goes back to "following your heart" or learning to trust your instincts, your intuition, and listen to the messages within. In other words, let go and let God - trusting that the answers you seek, the directions to follow, are right inside you. It requires listening and receiving them, and then taking action when you feel that tug on your heart, or you hear that voice in your head saying, "Go this way. Do that thing. Take that chance." That voice is your Higher Self, God, the Universe, whatever you want to call it.

Think of it this way: Your heart is like a radio receiver, tuning into your Higher Self, as if you were tuning your radio into the signal being broadcast by a radio station. To carry this analogy a little further, radio and TV stations frequently broadcast tornado warnings. If you live in an area affected by the warning, it's important to listen to that message and take action by staying away from the windows, or pulling over to the side of the road and seeking cover if you're in a car. Otherwise, you could get seriously hurt if you wind up in the path of that tornado.

In the same way, I believe ignoring the messages from your Higher Self puts your physical and mental health at risk. There have been too many times in my own life when I ignored my intuition and I regretted it. Regret leads to anger, frustration, stress and in some cases, even depression.

I have certainly felt anger, frustration and stress plenty of times in my life. But the closest I ever came to depression was when I was a teenager and I briefly considered committing suicide to escape the emotional turmoil I was in. Some of that was normal teenage angst that we all go through when our hormones start raging. But it was also my family environment, and years of being bullied by kids at school and in the neighborhood, who would call me names like Fatso, or would snatch the hat off my head in the winter and play "keep away" by throwing it back and forth to each other, just out of my reach.

I believe the reason I'm here today is because God had bigger plans for me, even though I didn't know that when I was a teenager. While "life with my dad (and mom) wasn't ever a picnic," as the song, "At the Ballet" from the musical *A Chorus Line* goes, I knew killing myself was not the answer. I may have had a love/hate relationship with my mom, but one of the memories that got etched into my brain as a seven-year-old was seeing how devastated she was when her best friend committed suicide. I knew I could not put my mom through that ordeal.

Thankfully, I have never felt sad or depressed long enough that it seriously interfered with my life. I never felt compelled to stay home from work because I could not face the world, for example. Despite my upbringing, I am generally a positive person; one who sees the glass as half-full, rather than half-empty. I believe that is why I have never had any serious health problems, even when I was obese. I do not suffer from high blood pressure or diabetes. On the other hand, I believe that stress and depression led to the health problems that caused my parents' and siblings' early transition from this life. That belief is grounded in medical evidence:

Stresses arising from alterations in our external environment, including emotional stress derived from interpersonal relationships, have been shown to be involved in the genesis of internal organ disease. For example, there is ample evidence to suggest that stress plays an important role in the pathogenesis of gastroduodenal ulcers, high blood pressure, and sudden cardiac death. -- "Neurocardiology - Anatomical and Functional Principles" by J. Andrew Armour, MD, PhD

My dad, who abused alcohol, and smoked cigarettes, died from a heart attack at age 68. My mom, who struggled with depression and obesity, passed at age 78 from heart disease. My brother, who abused alcohol and smoked pot regularly, died of atherosclerosis (hardening of the arteries) at 33. And finally, my sister, who suffered from bouts of depression, died from cancer at 64.

Quite the lineage, huh? I am grateful to be in my late 50s and intend to make it to my 100s with a healthy body, mind, and spirit. The reason I believe it is possible is because God loves me - and YOU - and keeps sending me help. Sometimes I took advantage of the help without recognizing that the Universe was sending it to me for a higher purpose. For instance, several years ago I was offered a discount to attend Tony Robbins' Unleash the Power Within workshop where I walked on hot coals! That activity required me to let go of the not unreasonable belief that stepping on hot coals would burn my feet, and it required me to open my heart to trust that God would keep me and my feet safe.

Talk about a radical idea. That experience helped me grow as a person, to see that I could change the thoughts and beliefs in my head, and choose new ones. I believed that my feet would be fine, and they were! Unfortunately, my old "not enough" beliefs came back soon after attending this workshop because I had not yet received and begun applying the L.O.V.E. principles I am sharing with you here.

Even though I wanted to make a change, I was still blocking what I wanted unconsciously. How do I know? I only had to look around at my life. Despite my upbeat persona, I was not as happy, fulfilled, and successful as I wanted to be. If you're not getting the results you want in life, it's likely because you believe you don't deserve it because you are harboring one of those "I'm not enough" or "I'm not worthy" stories.

I'm not expecting you to get rid of those beliefs this instant just because you're reading this book. You could. It is within your power to change your mind and start thinking new, empowering thoughts right now which will turn into beliefs when you think them long enough.

The reality is that it will likely take some time. What will speed the process up is for you to put your trust in your Higher Power. When you do, you will be able to see new possibilities for your life and your business or career open before you. New ideas will pop into your head when you least expect it. You may be in the shower when it happens, or during a meditation. I love it when that happens to me. Those ideas are the best. I call them divine downloads. It's how this book showed up in my head.

Keeping an open heart and mind means allowing yourself to receive new opportunities in your business, new avenues for growth and even new relationships – either personally or professionally. I know it can be scary taking a leap of faith and placing your trust in something you cannot see. But it's worth it. Think back to times in your life when you've been bold and taken action. I suspect the results were totally worth it. Most big risks deliver a big payoff.

One of the biggest risks I have taken in my business was investing in that year-long coaching and training course to run masterminds that I mentioned earlier. When the opportunity came to invest in the LEAD program, I knew in my heart that this was the path I needed to follow. The program provided facilitator training and the experience of being in a mastermind, so I would know what it would be like to run one myself. However, this program cost more than $10K – more money than I had ever spent on a program for my business.

I knew in my heart that I had to invest in LEAD. That's not to say I wasn't scared. My ego was screaming in my head! But I managed the fear with a few deep breaths, and the conviction in my heart and soul that I had to do this.

And I was right. That decision has paid dividends in so many ways in my personal life and my business. I'm convinced now that God wanted me to be in LEAD so I could receive the mastermind training and personal development coaching that was included. Those programs, along with the L.O.V.E. Method, enabled me to reframe my limiting beliefs, invigorate my spirituality, and redirect my business in a way that allows me to help my clients tap into their higher power so they can be more authentic online, and more successful in their businesses.

Remember my story about Show and Tell? I was sitting in an airport waiting for my flight home after attending one of the LEAD personal development workshops. As I was journaling to pass the time, that second grade memory came back to me. With the new information I'd learned during the weekend, it occurred to me that I may have totally misinterpreted Timothy's speech during Show and Tell. He may have secretly liked my attention, and decided to get up in class to brag about it! It was only my limiting belief about worthiness that caused me to assume he was making fun of me. And as my mother used to say, "Never assume because it makes an ass out of you and me."

What neuroplasticity demonstrates is that I can rewrite history as far as my brain is concerned. It doesn't matter which version of this story "really" happened. It's in the past. I get to decide on a new, more empowering story, and I get to decide how I reacted to this new, past story. I now imagine that when Timothy told his story, I stood up straight in class, and beamed with pride, because I knew Timothy liked me. I use this memory as proof that I AM worthy. That people do love me. And that I am lovable. I can believe it because my brain does not know the difference. And neither does yours.

Being open to receive is the pathway to having more of what you want, especially love and joy and abundance. When we're not open, we're closed off and push away the things that the Universe wants to give us. The minute we can relax and be open and receptive to our Higher Power, that is when the things we want begin to flow towards us, just like opening a faucet will let the water flow out.

CHAPTER 8

CONNECTING WITH YOUR HIGHER POWER

So far, I've talked about opening your heart to receive love, compliments, money and new opportunities. I saved the best concept for last and that is "Opening Your Heart to Receive God."

I know God has a sense of humor and a sense of irony because as I write this chapter, I'm listening to Pandora. The song that is playing is one I have sung in church. It is called *Open the Eyes of My Heart* by Michael W. Smith, and includes these simple, yet powerful lyrics:

> Open the eyes of my heart, Lord
> Open the eyes of my heart
> I want to see You
> I want to see You

Why would business owners or anyone else for that matter, want to open their heart to receive God? And what does opening your heart to receive God really mean?

Here's where I want to talk about faith again. This time we will refer to Merriam-Webster's definition: "Belief and trust in and loyalty to God."

I've always had faith in God. I just haven't had faith in the Catholic Church. I often felt like a hypocrite during mass, and as a result, I couldn't fully embrace God's message. It got lost in translation, so to speak. The message got covered up with all the pronouncements about guilt and sin and not being worthy. It's a shame because I wasted a lot of time and energy feeling bad about myself, instead of focusing on what I instinctively knew was the truth – that I am worthy and deserve all the best life has to offer. There's a section in the New Testament, Matthew 6:25-34, where Jesus explains this:

"Therefore I tell you, do not worry about your life, what you will eat or what you will drink, or about your body, what you will wear. Is not life more than food, and the body more than clothing? Look at the birds of the air: they neither sow nor reap nor gather into barns, and yet your heavenly Father feeds them. **Are you not of more value than they?** And can any of you by worrying add a single hour to your span of life? And why do you worry about clothing? Consider the lilies of the field, how they grow: they neither toil nor spin, yet I tell you, even Solomon in all his glory was not clothed like one of these. But if God so clothes the grass of the field, which is alive today and tomorrow is thrown into the oven, will he not much more clothe you - you of little faith? Therefore do not worry, saying, 'What will we eat?' or 'What will we drink?' or 'What will we wear?' For it is the Gentiles who strive for all these things; and indeed your heavenly Father knows that you need all these things. But strive first for the kingdom of God and his righteousness, and all these things will be given to you as well. "So do not worry about tomorrow, for tomorrow will bring worries of its own. Today's trouble is enough for today. *(boldness added for emphasis)*

My interpretation of this scripture passage is that we are more valuable than the birds in the air, (and animals on the ground, even though they're not mentioned specifically in this passage.) If we seek God first, everything we want, all of our desires, will be given to us. It is no wonder that one of the favorite songs I used to sing in our church choir was called, *Don't Worry About Tomorrow* which incorporated much of that passage in its lyrics. (Listen to the Immanuel CSI Church Choir sing it on YouTube: https://youtu.be/PHUHXXc2xA0

Opening your heart to receive God is a way to open your heart to love. The Bible says God is love. I'm going to step out of traditional Christian theology here and tap into what some religious leaders would call a heretical thought, and that is my belief that I am God and you are God. That means opening your heart to receive God is opening your heart to receive yourself. It's embracing who you are at a divine, spiritual level. (I'm going to address this in more detail later in the book.) This isn't my ego talking either. There are two passages in the New Testament where Jesus affirms this.

1. "He who abides in love abides in God, and God in him." (1 John 4:16)

2. "The Kingdom of God is within you." (Luke 17:21)

I'm not sure who originally said this, but I believe it to be true: we are spiritual beings living a human existence. We are all connected energetically, so when we let go of our limiting beliefs and open our hearts to receive God, we will have all the strength and the love we need to reach the hearts and minds of our prospects and clients.

There's a popular meme attributed to Mahatma Gandhi that says, "Be the change you wish to see in the world." That's a worthwhile message, and it doesn't go far enough to reflect the true power of what this remarkable leader actually said:

"If we could change ourselves, the tendencies in the world would also change. As a man changes his own nature, so does the attitude of the world change towards him. This is the divine mystery supreme. A wonderful thing it is and the source of our happiness. We need not wait to see what others do." – Mahatma Gandhi

My intention with this 2nd principle of the L.O.V.E. Method, the exercises that follow, and the rest of this book is to help you change your nature, so you can change the world in a positive way. We've got to start somewhere, right?

L.O.V.E. PRACTICES

Rewrite Your Story

Remember how I changed my perspective about the Show and Tell incident into one in which I imagined that Timothy was bragging to the class that I was trying to kiss him? That's an example of how you can rewrite a memory that reflects a limiting belief into a memory that's empowering. Here's how you can go about doing this.

- #1 - Describe an early memory that makes you sad or angry to think about.
- #2 - Describe what limiting belief about yourself that memory evokes.
- #3 - Rewrite the memory to create a happy ending.
- #4 - Describe what empowering belief that new ending has created for you.

Here's what this looks like with my Show and Tell story:

- #1 - Timothy tells class I'm chasing him around the playground to kiss him. Everyone laughs and I feel embarrassed.

#2 - I'm not worthy to be loved.

#3 - Timothy brags to the class that I want to kiss him. I sit up straight and smile because I'm proud of it!

#4 - I love myself and I enjoy showing other people that I care about them too.

Receive Praise

When someone pays you a compliment, pause for a moment, and then say, "Thank you!" Resist the temptation to offer them a compliment in return. You can always do that another time. For now, just bask in the praise. Receive it and hold it in your heart.

Ask for What You Want

One of the best ways to get used to asking for help is to spend one day doing it consistently. Pretend that you are a Queen or King and spend a day asking people to do things for you. As an example, when you are watching TV with a friend or family member, for instance, rather than getting up and going in the kitchen yourself to get something to eat or drink, ask someone to get it for you. If you get pushback, tell them your coach wants you to do this as an experiment, and to please humor you. I did this with my family once. It felt weird at first, but it was nice to be pampered that way for a change. It has made it easier for me to ask for help when I need it.

Connect with God

There are a variety of ways you can choose to connect with God. Meditation, as I've mentioned before, is an excellent way to get started.

You might feel close to God in nature, so spend time in the woods or at the beach. Go for a walk. Open your mind and heart and listen for the voice within. Don't be afraid to ask for help.

I highly recommend reading and applying the lessons in *A Course in Miracles*. You can study the lessons on your own or study under the direction of a spiritual coach who specializes in ACIM. Or you can read Alan Cohen's book, *A Course in Miracles Made Easy*.

You can also choose to connect with God at a house of prayer, such as a church, synagogue, mosque or community center. There is no right or wrong way to do this. Just know that God is here for you 24/7!

PART 3

VALUE YOUR UNIQUENESS

"To be yourself in a world that is constantly trying to make you something else is the greatest accomplishment." — Emerson

CHAPTER 9

FINDING THE COURAGE TO BE YOU

My mom used to call me a child of God. I know she believed that because she named me Gloria Grace! I believe that we are all children of God; we are connected to Source and have that divine spark within us. And just as no two snowflakes are alike, we are all unique creatures. Even identical twins are not exactly the same; there can be slight variations in each twin's genetic makeup. Why is it important to value our uniqueness, and why do many of us have trouble doing so?

I believe it comes back to those limiting beliefs we have talked about - especially those feelings of "I'm not enough" and "I'm not worthy." These beliefs have been prominent in my life, so much so that it has interfered with my ability to value my unique talents, abilities and experiences that have shaped who I am. For many people, the "I'm not worthy" belief is unconscious. But as a Catholic, I had this belief reinforced for me every Sunday at mass! Before receiving Communion, the congregation recited the following prayer: "Lord, *I am not worthy* to receive you, but only say the word, and my soul shall be healed."

A few years ago, the prayer was changed to "Lord, I am not worthy that you should enter under my roof, but only say the word, and my soul shall be healed." The new wording comes from Matthew 8:8 in the Bible. It is a response from a Centurion to Jesus, after Jesus said he would come and cure the man's paralyzed servant.

I did not pay attention to the significance of those words until about ten years ago when I heard a comedian make a joke about this language. Something clicked inside of me, because from then on, I felt uncomfortable saying it. Eventually, I stopped saying it altogether because my soul knew those words were not the truth. I AM worthy, and so are you! We are all worthy because we are alive, and we are created in God's image.

I believe this phrase was taken out of context by the Catholic Church to reinforce the concept that "we are sinners" and we need forgiveness by God before we can even hope to go to heaven.

But there is no basis for that in the Bible. Matthew doesn't claim that Jesus says in response to the Centurion, "You're right. You aren't worthy to have me in your house to heal your servant." No. Matthew states that Jesus said to his followers that he was amazed at the man's faith, and he told the Centurion, "Go; let it be done for you according to your faith."

While I know that I am worthy today, it takes effort to reprogram 50+ years of Catholic indoctrination. As a result, I still have my moments of doubt. They cropped up again while writing this book. As I pulled together my notes, I discovered that the "Value Your Uniqueness" section had the least amount of content because, clearly, this was the area that needed my attention the most. I am going to do my best to explain why this subject is important to me, and why I feel it is important to you too. In this and the following chapters, you will learn what to do to start appreciating your value, and how to find the courage to demonstrate it in the world. One thing that is not unique about me, is that I know I am not the only one who has trouble in this area!

What other reasons could there be to explain why we do not value our uniqueness? I think it's reflective of our culture. Society and peer pressure to conform starts when we are kids, and so we start to dim our light to fit in. We start fearing people who are different from us, either in the way they look or the beliefs they hold. And this fear leads to conflict, violence, and war – you only have to look back at 2020 with the Black Lives Matter movement, and the political division during and after the U.S. presidential election to see evidence of this. Imagine what the world would be like if instead of fearing everyone who was different from us, we embraced them as unique individuals who are worthy of our time and our love.

God bless the children who stand firm in their convictions and let their freak flags fly! They are blessed to have someone in their lives who says it's more important to be yourself than to go along with the crowd. Or those children may just be blessed with a strong inner sense of self that will not let them be persuaded to act, talk, or look a certain way to be accepted by the so-called "cool crowd." That pressure to fit in continues into adulthood. It's what leads to the pressure to "keep up with the Joneses." You see your neighbor go out and buy a new car or get a new flat screen TV, and now you want a new car and TV too.

It shows up on social media as well. Your friends post pictures of their latest vacation, and now you want to go somewhere fabulous too. Never mind that you can't afford it. It is where FOMO comes in - fear of missing out. It's really about the trap of comparing ourselves to others, which leads to what's called "imposter syndrome" - feeling that we don't measure up, and we aren't worth as much as the other person. In fact, according to a review article published in the

International Journal of Behavioral Science, studies have shown that an estimated 70% of people experience these impostor feelings at some point in their lives.

This was a trap I fell into as a business owner. I would look at the amount of revenues in my balance sheet, or lack thereof (!), and that would be disheartening enough. Then, I would see one of my entrepreneur friends post on social media that they had landed a huge client or were speaking at a major conference, and I would feel inadequate and a failure. I believed I "should" be farther along in my business and have more success.

Thankfully, I could call my sister and she would encourage me. She'd point out that I had accomplished a lot, and that I needed to lighten up on myself. With her passing, I lost my cheerleader. I had to find another way to let go of the comparison and focus on what I was accomplishing. Attending various personal development programs, and working with various coaches and counselors helped. But I still found myself slipping back into this "not enough" mentality. Which led me to journal the following:

Why are we so scared to be ourselves? Why are we afraid to own our value and tell people about it?

WE'RE AFRAID OF JUDGMENT. SOMEONE PROBABLY JUDGED US OR REJECTED US AND SO OUR BRAIN KEEPS REPLAYING THAT MEMORY OVER AND OVER AGAIN. LIKE A BROKEN RECORD. OR A TAPE ON A LOOP. OR MAYBE IT'S A VIRUS ON YOUR COMPUTER THAT HAS CORRUPTED YOUR HARDDRIVE. HOW DO WE FIX THAT HARD DRIVE IN OUR HEAD? CALL ON GOD THE ULTIMATE PC REPAIR PERSON. JUST NEED TO REBOOT. WHEN IN DOUBT REBOOT. ERASE THOSE OLD TAPES AND FEED NEW DATA INTO YOUR MEMORY BANKS. And then keep feeding it every day. Like a plant you give sunshine and water to help it grow. Your mind and spirit and soul need that attention always. Tell yourself, "I love you." Keep reminding yourself that you are worthy.

That preceding paragraph was the answer that came to me as I journaled at my computer, instead of handwriting in a notebook. I didn't even notice at first that I was typing with the caps lock on my keyboard. As I calmed down and saw what I had done, I took the caps lock off.

This is one of those times where I believe God was shouting at me to pay attention - LOL! The message is important for me and for you, which is why I decided to reproduce it here for you to see it the way I originally wrote it.

As I've already mentioned, our old limiting beliefs will keep replaying in our minds over and over again, keeping us stuck, until we become aware of them. When that happens, we can choose to stay stuck, or we can take action to move forward by coming up with new empowering beliefs and install those in our brain instead.

CHAPTER 10

THE COST OF NOT VALUING YOUR WORTH

"If you doubt your power, you give power to your doubt."
Diane von Furstenberg

Let's get back to the bigger question - Why is it important that we value ourselves? For one simple reason, if we don't, how the hell can we expect anyone else to value who we are, or what we do? It might be useful to look at the definitions of value and uniqueness:

Value:

estimate the monetary worth of (something). consider (someone or something) to be important or beneficial; have a high opinion of.

Uniqueness:

the quality of being the only one of its kind.

the quality of being particularly remarkable, special, or unusual.

Business owners and self-employed professionals who have the "I'm not enough" story running in their heads often run into problems pricing their services. I can't tell you how many hours I've spent agonizing over how much to charge. What wound up happening was that I charged too little for what I did. And I know many other entrepreneurs, especially women in the healing professions, who struggle in this area too. I get it. You don't want to turn away anyone who needs your services. And… it's important to remember that as a business owner, you have bills to pay just like everyone else. You must place a high value on what you do, and charge accordingly.

Remember my sister's reluctance to accept that holiday gift? Deep down, Michaela didn't value herself; she didn't value her skills and knowledge enough to feel that she was worthy of such a generous gift.

I believe that failure to own her value kept my sister from believing she could be successfully treated for cancer. Michaela expressed frustration with the cancer and her limiting beliefs in a journal entry she made after learning that four months of chemotherapy treatments had failed to shrink the tumor. These are her words:

"So - interesting… I say I want to stay alive, yet I totally doubt the treatment can help me. I feel condemned and am operating on life's not fair and I'm screwed again. So, basically, how I'm responding to the whole cancer thing is based on one or more of my beliefs about life - that I always get dealt a bad hand, raw deal, etc. I discount hope. For me, having this "special" cancer and having trouble tolerating the treatment is more evidence of life sucks and then you die. I seem to assume that suffering is what I get in life… need to work more on this. Clue: resisting believing that treatment could actually work, and I would get a few good years."

One reason why I decided to include her comments in this chapter is because I was having my own crisis of faith regarding my value while writing this section of the book. One afternoon, I attended an online networking meeting where I had to say what I specialized in.

During a breakout session with a few other attendees, I talked about my SEO copywriting business, and then the others gave me their feedback. One lovely woman said she understood what I did and wondered if there was something else I wanted to say. I mentioned that I had a podcast and was writing a book about how to live fully, love deeply and engage authentically. And she said, "Oh. That's what you're passionate about!"

I was hiding my light again and after the call I got down on myself for it. I started questioning why I could not express that. After a good cry, I journaled about why I was in such a funk… and decided that it was because it had been four years since I received that call from a nurse at a Tucson hospital urging me to fly out immediately to be with Michaela because of the bowel obstruction she had suffered. I decided to dig through a box of my sister's papers to find out the exact date she had been admitted to the hospital. That is when I found her notebook and read the entry I included above.

Remember in Part 2 of this book, when I talked about opening your heart to receive inspiration and guidance? This is an example of what that looks like. I followed this inner guidance, which I believe was from my sister, directing me to find that notebook. She wanted to tell me that the negative beliefs we hold onto do us no good, and believing that suffering is what we get in life is a faulty assumption! It also served as a reminder for me to take to heart the quote I have taped to my desk from *A Course in Miracles*. It says, "I am as God created me. His Son can suffer nothing. And I AM His Son." (W-p. II. 110.6.3)

What is the cost of failing to value your uniqueness? It harms your self-esteem. It keeps you from shining your light fully in the world. When you don't value the unique knowledge, skills, abilities and experience you bring to the world, it becomes easy to hide in plain sight. And in practical business terms, if you can't convey why someone should do business with you, those potential customers will find someone else, taking their money with them.

I used to find it ironic that the SEO copywriting business I started involved me helping other clients to demonstrate what makes them unique so they could attract, engage, and convert leads into sales. Now, I know it is just an example of the fact that it is easier to do for others, what I had trouble doing for myself – letting people know what is unique about me! Case in point – it took me over a year to update the messaging on my own website, something it takes me a couple of weeks to do for one of my clients!

This also became evident when I worked with a branding specialist to position myself more effectively with my ideal clients and create a "big brand" for my company that would stand out from my competition.

Since I had been in business for 11 years at the time, it should have been a no-brainer for me to come up with an answer to the question, "What's unique about me and my business?" But I got stuck. So, I did something about it. When I get tripped up like this, I ask myself why and start journaling. I wrote down the following question: "Why am I having trouble coming up with what's unique about me?" That question sparked a realization that the most likely culprit was fear. Fear of being seen, fear of being criticized, fear of making mistakes.

Then I searched my mind to see what was in my past that might have caused me to doubt myself like this and not value my uniqueness. One of the memories that came to mind took place when I was in the 8th grade. It was 1976, the year the United States celebrated its bicentennial. I had a reputation in school as an excellent speller. In fact, I had won the school spelling bee in 5th grade and again in 7th grade. My classmates figured there was an excellent chance I would win again that year. I hoped so too because I wanted another chance to compete at the District level, where the winner would advance to compete for the State Spelling Bee Championship.

As fate would have it, the very first word I had to spell during the bee in 1976, was "bicentennial." And I got it wrong! Going out on the very first word was bad enough, but to have it be "bicentennial" was the icing on a horrible-tasting cake! That word was everywhere – in the newspaper, billboards, television commercials, you name it - and I was furious with myself for missing it. The guys in school gave me a hard time about it too. As a result, the story I made up about that event was that if you make a mistake people are going to tease you and criticize you. It is better to be quiet and not shine your brilliance in the world.

This story made perfect sense to me as to why I was having such trouble communicating what's unique about me, and why someone should do business with me. I was afraid that if I made a mistake, I would be criticized for it. Growing up, my parents yelled at me for making mistakes. So, there was past evidence to justify my fear.

There is an expression that says, "past performance is no guarantee of future results." I have often seen this statement regarding financial investments. But in this case, I believed my past performance WAS a strong predictor of future results. Subconsciously, I was afraid that the next time I made a mistake, it would expose me as a fraud, someone who didn't know what they were doing, and certainly didn't merit being in business, let alone succeeding in business!

Wow. Talk about damned if you do, and damned if you don't. The thing is… this fear was NOT justified at all now that I was an adult. As a business owner, I've been successful in helping my clients achieve their goals. And on the rare occasions when I have made a mistake, I have owned up to it right away, and no client has ever yelled at me, criticized me, or even left me a poor review!

I love this message from *A Course in Miracles*, which teaches: "The only value that the past can hold is that you learn it gave you no rewards that you would want to keep. For only thus would you be willing to relinquish it and have it gone forever." (T-25. C.1:7)

When I came upon this passage, it made such sense to me. It's important to look at our past beliefs and see them for what they are: attack thoughts. We beat ourselves up by holding on to these "I'm not worthy" beliefs when they are the farthest thing from the truth. We are unique individuals, designed in God's image, and therefore, invaluable! When you own that, it becomes that much easier to share who you are, and to speak your truth so you can engage authentically with your family, friends, and clients / co-workers.

What is your truth? It's your essence. It's the sum total of your talents, skills, abilities, experience, knowledge, and the beliefs you have about them. To value your uniqueness, then, means to appreciate all of those things and know that they are what makes you who you are at this very moment. And yet, here is the stumbling block we run into. The things we excel at, the things that come easy for us to do, are what we often take for granted. And as a consequence, we don't mention them in conversation. Or we downplay them on our company website. We do not value them, and as a result, we are not honoring the value we bring into the world. Instead, we go around like Clark Kent with amnesia, not knowing his true identity is Superman! And to carry the analogy further, just as Superman's powers can be diminished by Kryptonite, our "kryptonite" is the limiting belief that we're not worthy. And as Superman's powers diminish when he's surrounded by that glowing rock, we too, are metaphorically pinned to the floor, unable to get up and do our job effectively, whether that's running a business or a family.

Sometimes we have to hear something over and over again in order for us to get the message that we need to value our uniqueness. And sometimes, God whacks us over the head with a metaphorical 2x4 when we're slow to get that message! That's what happened to me on Wednesday, December 19, 2018.

CHAPTER 11

SYNCHRONICITIES AND HEALTH SCARES

In December 2018, I had been working with a coach for nearly a year to help me grow my business. While working together, we wound up focusing on my relationship with God. My coach, Michael, had been encouraging me to speak publicly about what I believed, to value my spiritual essence and let it shine in the world. Since I was developing this book at the time, I started giving presentations about the L.O.V.E. Method. They were well received, and the more I spoke about God, love, and the lessons I have shared so far in this book, the happier and more fulfilled I felt.

And yet… it was not until that coaching session in December, when it finally dawned on me WHY I was given the L.O.V.E. Method to write about: I had to learn and apply these lessons for myself. That revelation hit me like a ton of bricks. As soon as the call ended, I sat on the floor of my office and cried my eyes out. It seems so obvious to me now, because in life, we often teach what we need to learn. To write the book, I had to KNOW this material in my soul. And God knew these lessons would help me ease my grief over losing my sister.

After a good long cry, I dried my tears, grabbed some lunch, and got in my car to drive to a singing lesson. I love to sing. My favorite thing about attending Girl Scout camp when I was a kid was singing around the campfire. I had sung in several church choirs over the years, but I had never taken formal voice lessons. Even though I was not singing in a choir at the time, I still wanted the experience, and I also figured it would help with public speaking too, since I frequently give presentations for my business.

I had only been driving for about five minutes, when it suddenly occurred to me that I did not know where I was going. Not in the sense that I didn't know how to get there. I had been taking voice lessons at the same location for a few weeks already. My problem was that I did not know WHY I was in the car in the first place! This panicky feeling came over me. I kept asking myself, "Why am I in this car? Where am I going? What am I doing?" I started freaking out, thinking that I was having a stroke. I pulled into a shopping center, parked my car at the back of the lot, turned off the engine and noticed the sheet music sitting next to me for my voice lesson. I remember looking at it and asking out loud, "What is that for? Why do I have music in the car?" I had no idea what was going on, where I was going, or why. I was consumed with fear. It was the freakiest feeling in the world, and one I never hope to have again! Despite this memory loss, I still had the presence of mind to get my cellphone out of my purse and call my daughter for help.

What I learned later on was that I didn't just call my daughter once. I called her six times and said the exact same thing every time. It freaked her out just a little bit - LOL! I also called my husband, who was at work, which I do not remember doing at all. The next thing I do remember was seeing a fire rescue truck pull alongside of me, and an EMT walk over to my car to ask me how I was doing. I told him what was going on, and he recommended that I let them take me to the ER to get checked out, which I did.

By the time I got to the hospital, my memory was coming back, and I realized that I had been on my way to my voice lesson, and I was disappointed that I missed it! After an hour or so in the hospital, getting examined and the doctors not finding anything dire going on, they let me go home, with the recommendation that I schedule a follow-up MRI, CAT scan and all that fun stuff. After the tests were completed, I went back to my doctor for a follow-up consultation where I found out all the results were normal. My doctor thought I had experienced Transient Global Amnesia (TGA), which is a sudden, temporary episode of memory loss that is not harmful, and cannot be attributed to a more common neurological condition, such as epilepsy or stroke. My doctor reassured me that I would most likely never experience it again, for which I am eternally grateful!

Doctors do not understand what causes TGA, but they do know some of the triggers include emotional distress or psychological stress, and strenuous physical activity. TGA also typically occurs in people over the age of 50, and who have a history of migraines. I was 56 when this occurred. Check. I had a history of migraines. Check. The weekend before the incident, I had completed a half marathon. Check. And an hour before the episode, I had undergone a major emotional breakthrough with my coach. CHECK!

It still took me a few months after that incident before I finally sat down to begin writing the book. In the process of writing, I have had to redo these lessons for myself several times. But that is the good thing about being human. Life is a journey and sometimes we take a few steps backward before we can make major leaps forward. It is natural to go back a bit to get perspective and then when you know where you are going, you can take that leap and hit the mark. I am ok with taking a few steps backwards because I am always going to move forward. I will not allow myself to stay stuck and neither should you. The good news about implementing the practices in this book is that they have helped me to recover quickly when I start to feel bad or judge myself harshly for making a mistake. Now, I can bounce back from those feelings within minutes, as opposed to hours or days like before. This is all part of the growth process.

I believe we are here on this Earth to learn and to grow and to serve. And if you are ready to do the same, you believe it too. Even if you are not conscious of it. There is a stirring in your soul; and if I can help ignite that spark within you, I will be utterly grateful to God for the gift I have been given to share. As I wrote that sentence, the song "We Are Many Parts" by Marty Haugin popped into my head. The refrain goes, "We are many parts, we are all one body. And the gifts we have we are given to share. May the spirit of love make us one indeed. One the love that we share. One our hope in despair. One the cross that we bear."

Coincidence or Divine Timing?

When I decided to write about my amnesia incident for this book, I got curious about the exact date when it happened. (Evidence of my intuition / Higher Power at work again.) I thought it had taken place in December, so I checked my Google calendar and saw that the episode happened on Wednesday, Dec. 19, a week before Christmas. In that moment, a light bulb went off in my head. That's because a week before my sister transitioned in December, 2016, she and I had spent the day in Phoenix - with her enduring a four-hour round-trip car ride from Tucson - to talk with a doctor about a radiation treatment called CyberKnife.

CyberKnife is a non-invasive treatment that delivers precise high-dose radiation treatment to a tumor, while minimizing damage to the surrounding healthy tissue. My husband had learned about CyberKnife while researching cancer treatments after Michaela got diagnosed, and I had been trying for months to get her in for an evaluation to see if she was a good candidate for it.

Michaela had hoped chemotherapy would reduce the tumor's size enough for a surgeon to remove it. She had treatments for about a year, and at first, the tumor responded and started to shrink. But then the chemo stopped doing the job it was intended to do. Instead, all it did was kill off my sister's healthy white blood cells, which took longer and longer to recover after each treatment. Finally, Michaela had enough and stopped chemo altogether. By the time she finally agreed to try CyberKnife in the fall of 2016, it then took me weeks to get her medical records sent from Tucson up to Phoenix. It was a relief to finally have an appointment on the schedule for us to attend. Even though Michaela was in hospice care at this point, I was still hoping for a miracle to save my sister's life, or at least prolong it.

That Phoenix trip was significant for a couple of reasons. For one thing, the doctor gave us hope! He did not believe the CyberKnife treatment would get rid of the tumor altogether, but he was quite confident that it could improve the quality of her life by reducing her pain level. That would enable Michaela to stop, or significantly reduce, the dosage of the potent painkillers she was on, which included Fentanyl and Morphine. We left Phoenix feeling optimistic, with the plan being that she would start treatment after the New Year.

Unfortunately, by the time we got back home to Tucson two hours later, my sister was exhausted. She had trouble getting out of the car to go into the house. She slept most of the next day. It turned out that the appointment came too late for her. Michaela started a downward spiral that culminated in her passing five days later.

Realizing that these two events - our trip to Phoenix and the revelation that I needed to learn the L.O.V.E. Method - came exactly two years apart was mind blowing to me. It reinforced for me that there are no coincidences in this world. Signs are all around us if we are willing to see them. Also, this recognition gave me a beautiful example to include in this book. As for the amnesia episode itself, I took it to be a loving "knock upside the head" from God to make sure I truly understood I needed to learn how to Let Go and Let God, Open My Heart to Receive Love, Value My Uniqueness and Embrace My Divinity (which we will cover in the final section of the book).

When it came to valuing my unique qualities, I had to learn how to value more than my talents and abilities. I had to value another unique aspect of myself that we all share: our emotions.

CHAPTER 12

WHAT'S LOVE (AND FEAR) GOT TO DO WITH IT?

I trust by now that you have learned why it is important for us to value our uniqueness. But how do we DO that, especially if we are afraid to shine our light in the world? Before I get to that, I want to talk about another aspect of ourselves that we often devalue: our feelings, our emotions. This is something I'm intimately familiar with because my feelings weren't something I trusted, or felt secure enough to show - especially the "negative" feelings of anger and frustration. I would bottle them up until there wasn't any more room to store them, and they would then burst out like a tidal wave in circumstances when all that was called for was a gentle wave of anger or disappointment. I would also stuff my feelings, quite literally with food. I did this because I dreaded confrontation. I didn't want to get into an argument. I grew up around so much yelling, that I hated fighting.

Early on in my marriage, my husband would get very angry about something and after exploding with a lot of yelling and cursing, he would then get very quiet and not talk for hours. This drove me crazy! If I was in the wrong, I would keep saying, "I'm sorry" in hopes that would get him to talk to me again. The longer he ignored me, the more guilty I felt, and the more anxious I felt. Subconsciously, I thought his anger must mean I was a bad person, and therefore, unlovable. And on the occasions when I felt his anger was unjustified because I believed I was "right" about a certain situation, I found myself apologizing to him anyway in the hopes that he would calm down and speak to me again. I eventually learned to give him space when he got angry, and let him calm down on his own without any interference on my part.

Looking back on those early days, it's clear we should have sought marriage counseling to learn how to manage disagreements, since I didn't get any guidance in this area from my parents. I had spent so much time running interference between my mom and dad as a kid -- "Tell your mom x-y-z." and "Tell your dad a-b-c." -- that I never found out how to manage conflict on my own. The only lesson I learned was that conflict should be avoided at all costs - even if I was the one paying the price. It was an example of how I was willing to give away my power because I didn't value myself enough to stand my ground, or even to seek help from a marriage expert. I settled, unconsciously believing that this was as good as it gets. Or that I didn't deserve any better treatment because I wasn't perfect. I made mistakes. And I should be punished for them. Even if the person doing the punishing was me!

Thankfully, there was a light within me that would "...not go gentle into that good night," as the poet Dylan Thomas said. God kept leading me to books, programs, people, and processes like the L.O.V.E. Method that enabled me to recognize the light within, nurture it, and allow it to burst forth from me into the world in the form of live presentations, videos, blog posts, emails, workshops, and ultimately, this book.

Writing this book has been a great awakening process for me because as I went through the editing process, I realized that the emotion I talked about at the start of this chapter was fear, not anger. I have heard experts say that there are only two basic human emotions: love and fear. Everything else stems from these. To value our uniqueness, it is important to value love and fear. These emotions teach us about ourselves.

I have spent a lot of time in this book talking about negative experiences and negative emotions, and how my inability to express myself kept me from living fully, loving deeply, and engaging authentically in my life and business. I do not want you to think that my life has been one long unhappy story. There have been a lot of positive things that have happened to me, including giving birth to an amazing daughter and son, who taught me a lot about myself during the last 20+ years. Until the idea for this book came about, my life had a lot of ups and downs because I was not being true to me. I was busy fulfilling others' expectations of who I "should" be.

Once I committed to writing this book, a transformation began to happen in my life. I started asking those major life questions of, "Who am I?" and "Why am I here?" and much to my surprise, I began to get answers. That act of saying, "Yes," to God enabled me to learn how to love myself (which I will talk more about in the final section of this book), and to value my unique emotions, talents, and abilities.

What are those talents? You may have already noticed that music is important to me. As the pandemic raged in 2020, the lockdown presented me with opportunities to return to my musical roots. In working with my coach, Marty, she had me make a list of my talents and abilities, as well as the things that bring me joy. That list included things like my ability to sing, and to play the organ, guitar, flute, and saxophone. I also like to write, of course! All through the year, I continued to spend every morning in meditation, which helped to center me and keep me grounded. One day, I pulled my guitar out of my closet where it had been sitting for 15 years, and I started to play again. I also wrote a couple of songs, something I had not done since I was 7 years old!

I share this with you not to brag, but to inspire you to take stock of what areas of life in which you excel, examine what your talents are, and to start doing what brings you joy. Along the way, you will undoubtedly feel fear. And that is ok too. Fear is our ego's way of protecting us. The goal of life is not to give in to the fear. There is an expression that says, "Feel the fear and do it anyway." There is a lot of merit to that. Stepping through the fear and stepping out of your comfort zone is how we grow. Anytime I have taken a big leap of faith, it has led to a big reward. I am not necessarily talking money here. (Although sometimes it has!) Often, it has generated a tremendous feeling of accomplishment, knowing that what I was afraid of was not that bad after all, and it proved that I was more resilient than I had thought. And that is a positive emotion to value!

L.O.V.E. PRACTICES

Here are a few ways you can start valuing what makes you unique!

Talent List

Write down a minimum of 10 things that you find easy to do. Include qualities about yourself that you like, such as you're friendly, you don't give up easily, etc. If you get stuck, ask someone close to you to share what they think you are good at, what they like about you, and add it to the list if it is not there already. Review this list whenever you have the inclination to compare yourself to others, or when you feel you're not good enough. It will remind you that you are an awesome, unique individual!

Testimonial List

Every time a client sends you a testimonial or writes a positive review about your business online, thank them right away (or as soon as you are aware of the comment), and then put the testimonial in your journal, and post them on your website as social proof! If you are an employee, keep track of positive comments your boss makes about you and your performance. If you can get a copy of your annual review, highlight your strengths in the report. Also, keep track of any positive reviews and recommendations you receive on social media sites like Facebook and LinkedIn. On those days when you feel down, and believe you are not worthy, re-read the comments. They will help raise your vibration, and make you feel good!

Journal

Buy a notebook, and write in it whenever you start to have doubts about your value and self-worth. While typing on the computer can be a valid way for some people to journal, writing by hand gives you an opportunity to visually express your feelings in the way you write. I am not talking word choices here. I am talking the size of the characters, or how messy or neat your words look. When you look at what you have written later, your penmanship or lack thereof, will speak volumes about the emotions you felt at the time, that typewritten words on a computer cannot convey. Do not overthink when you write. Try to keep the pen moving over the page and express your feelings on paper to see what your Higher Self has to say about a particular subject. As you do this more frequently, you will find that you can nip any feelings of self-doubt in the bud and renew your faith in yourself.

PART 4

EMBRACE YOUR DIVINITY

*"I looked in temples, churches & mosques.
But I found the Divine within my heart."* - Rumi

CHAPTER 13

SPIRITUAL SOUL SEARCHING

My initiation into the Catholic church came as a baby when my parents had me baptized. The Catechism of the Catholic Church says the sacrament of baptism means that we are freed from sin and reborn as sons of God. It's not that we come into the world having done anything wrong. The sin that's being washed away is the "Original sin" committed by Adam and Eve in the Garden of Eden, when they disobeyed God. And therefore, according to St. Paul, all men were made sinners.

This belief is not unique to Catholics. It's something the church has in common with other Christian religions. And it's something I've come to see as inherently faulty. If we are raised as children to believe that we are sinners, then doesn't it make sense that many people will continue to sin? It's practically expected! That's why Catholics are encouraged to go to confession, to confess their sins and obtain pardon from God's mercy.

After I stopped attending mass at our local Catholic church, I started attending Unity services. Unity takes a different stand with regards to sin. The founders of this organization, Charles and Myrtle Fillmore, believed that, "Our essence is of God; therefore, we are inherently good. This God essence was fully expressed in Jesus the Christ." Imagine if everyone was raised to believe this way. Sure, we're still going to make mistakes, but our essence is good, not evil.

I believe we were born in God's image, and as Lesson 36 in *A Course in Miracles* teaches, "You are holy because your mind is part of God's. If your mind is part of God's you must be sinless, or a part of His Mind would be sinful." (W-pII. 36.1.2) This is a key lesson because to "Embrace Your Divinity" means to recognize that your inner spirit, your Higher Self is holy, divine, and ultimately, worthy to receive all the good that you desire.

This is what the three prior sections have been leading up to: acknowledging that you are worthy BECAUSE you are a child of God - a part of the omnipotent, omnipresent God. Therefore, doubting yourself is to doubt God. Embracing your divinity means loving yourself, as God loves you. It is only by loving yourself truly, madly, and deeply, that you can engage authentically with others, and love them as they are - children of God.

What does it mean to love yourself? It means to acknowledge who you are. And to be kind to yourself. Think about someone you love. Do you constantly belittle them, call them "stupid," and treat them like dirt? Or do you respect them, listen to them, and even do random acts of kindness for them? I imagine so. Now, think of yourself as the person you love most. Can you treat yourself with respect? Can you be kind to yourself? Can you rest when you need rest? Can you stop beating yourself up for mistakes, and instead, embrace them as lessons to be learned?

The more ways you can show yourself how much you care about yourself, the better you'll feel. The better you feel, the more likely it is that you will treat others better too. And a circle of love starts to vibrate around you, where everyone loves to be with you because you treat yourself as highly as you treat the ones you love.

Embracing your divinity also means to embrace everything and everyone in this world. Why? Because we are all connected. We are all part of God, every living creature and every person, especially the ones we don't like. The pandemic of 2020 showed us just how much damage we had brought upon our Earth and how it could be restored simply by quarantining ourselves in our homes. When this happened, the factories stopped polluting, so the air and water got cleaner and we remembered to care about each other again…. for a time anyway.

I mentioned this lesson from A Course in Miracles in a previous chapter, and it's worth mentioning again here. It says, "I am as God created me. His Son can suffer nothing. And I AM His Son." (W-pII. 110.6.3) When we do not recognize that we are a spiritual being, we operate instead from our ego. The ego wants to keep us safe, and that means going against what our Higher Self wants, which is to learn and grow.

In essence, the ego doesn't want us to listen to God. The ego wants to be in control of our actions. The ego doesn't trust God, or even remember God. The ego thinks it's in control so if we don't do what it wants, it feels threatened. That's what Dr. Wayne Dyer meant when he said ego stands for Edging God Out. The ego wants us to focus on It. The ego knows that if we listen to what God wants, we may step out of our comfort zone. And we may in fact get hurt. It really is trying to protect us. The problem with this is that we're never going to grow if we don't try new things, if we don't take chances. That's the only way we're ever going to live fully and love deeply. It's part of human nature to get hurt. We're here to get as much out of life as possible. If we stay in our own cocoon like the ego wants, we will never be able to live fully. We'll stay "safe" and unhappy even though our soul is screaming for us to do something more with our lives. It knows that we are here to be more, to do more, to have more.

And when we let the ego rule, we are giving up our power. We are rejecting God, and in essence, rejecting ourselves. This is where the "I'm not enough" and "I'm not worthy" crap comes from. It is all B.S. – a faulty Belief System!

My mom used to say, "God doesn't make junk." And she's right. God doesn't make junk because God isn't made of junk. God made the universe, the trees and plants and rivers and animals and human beings. What we believe, how we think, and how we act determines the life we lead. If we believe that we aren't inherently good, we won't think good thoughts, and our results will not be good. So that's where the shift has to take place. Our world depends on the human race coming to terms with our inherent goodness. No race is inferior to another. We all bleed the same. Our blood contains red and white blood cells. Therefore, we are all the same underneath our skin color, and underneath the culture, and beliefs we were raised in.

The renowned spiritual teachers of history - like Jesus, Buddha, Mohammed - all embodied the Christ essence as Richard Rohr talks about in his excellent book, *"The Universal Christ."* They were human beings, just like us. That means we have the same potential to embrace our divinity and express it in the world in a positive way. What we lack is the confidence, education, and the will to do it. God wants us to return to our divine nature, to embrace it, so we can co-create a better world than the one we are living in now. We have forgotten too long, and are in danger of making this planet uninhabitable. God is knocking on our door - sending us viruses like COVID-19, in hopes that we will answer the door and welcome God into our lives like a long-lost relative or friend. We can use our free will to be like the prodigal son, who squandered his inheritance, realized the error of his ways, and returned to the Father who loved him and cared for him and gave him everything he ever wanted, and more.

For many years, I did not like this story when it was told in church because I identified with the older brother who chose to remain home with his father and take care of everything. He was angry that the father welcomed his younger brother with open arms and a feast to celebrate his return. I could relate because I felt like I always had to be the "good daughter" and do everything my mother asked of me, whether I wanted to or not. And I was angry because I did not feel she appreciated me for it.

That was my ego talking. One of the blessings of becoming a mother was that I started to see things from the Father's point of view in the prodigal son story. I love my children unconditionally, even when they have made mistakes. It is interesting that many biblical scholars say the point of this story is that we must repent to win God's favor because the prodigal son tells his father that he has sinned against him, and then the father orders his servants to prepare a feast in celebration. But before the son ever confesses, it is clear to me that the father has already forgiven him. The Bible verse says, "But while he was still far off, his father saw him and was filled with compassion; he ran and put his arms around him and kissed him." *Luke 15:20*

Does that sound like God has to forgive us to love us? I would argue, no. God loves us unconditionally. The problem is that we spend too much time punishing ourselves for perceived wrongdoing when we could be extending ourselves much needed love.

CHAPTER 14

MISSING THE MARK

I was born under the Virgo astrological sign, whose traits include being analytical, organized and a perfectionist. I do like to analyze things, and I love being organized (not the actual doing of it). But one of my downfalls has been perfectionism, to the point of being hypercritical of myself and others. One of the challenges I had in learning to embrace my divinity was that I had to learn how to stop beating myself up for mistakes and to stop judging people for not living up to my standards. I had to embrace my humanity as well as embrace my divinity. And that required forgiving myself for my mistakes and for judging others. When I was active in the Catholic church, I would periodically go to confession to confess my sins and have the priest absolve me of them, which is supposed to guarantee God's forgiveness. In studying *A Course in Miracles*, I learned that we do not need forgiveness because we do not sin. In fact, when you look at the Hebrew and Greek origins of the word "sin," it means to "miss the mark." The reality, contrary to traditional Christian theology, is that God does not *need* to forgive us. We need to forgive ourselves.

Or do we?

In the process of revising this book, I meditated and journaled frequently. One afternoon, I sat at my computer and asked God what I needed to say about forgiveness. At first, I answered my own question. I wrote that the Bible talks about our need to forgive others to receive forgiveness from God. Then I realized that it is more important to forgive ourselves because when we do, we are forgiving others because we are all One.

I then posed the question, "Why do we *need* to forgive ourselves?" That is when I got an answer that was not from me, it was an answer coming through me from my Higher Self.

It said, "You don't need to forgive yourself. What you need to do is love yourself. The ego thinks it needs forgiveness because the ego deals in punishment, cause, and effect. Make a mistake, get punished. And then ask for forgiveness so you can be absolved of your sins."

For some reason, I then typed, "Is it the ego?"

And my Higher Self responded, "The ego isn't really the word we'd use."

I typed, "What word would you use?"

The response was, "Your lower self. The part of you that has forgotten you are one with God. We call it Isha."

I stopped at this point and immediately went to Google to look up the definition of Isha. Several different languages use this word, but the one from India seemed right and that definition was lord, ruler. I asked, "Why would you refer to this lower self by that name?"

The response was, "Because it's a way for you to understand that the lower part is ruling over you, keeping you from knowing or remembering God."

116 | *Gloria Grace Rand*

Knowing God is to know our self, our true Higher self that is made of love, because we are part of God. Therefore, it is important to love ourselves, even when we make mistakes, because that truly is how we can enter the kingdom of Heaven right here on earth.

The reason so much of the Bible deals with God as an entity that we must be fearful of is because I believe the early church wanted to be in control. Men wanted to be in control. And that's because they were focused on their ego, rather than truly following what God wanted for us. God doesn't want there to be controlling factions. God wants us to love one another as God loves us, and that means treating each other as God. Seeing the Christ in each other. When we can do that, we won't be obsessed with power, control, guilt, and fear. Rather, we will be focused on love, joy, happiness, and peace. That's the ultimate goal of life here on earth - creating heaven on earth where we live in harmony with one another. And it all begins with me. "Let peace begin with me. Let this be the moment now," as the song says.

How do we create peace for ourselves? We start by giving ourselves a break. One morning, I had a limited amount of time to get ready for a podcast interview I was going to record. I wanted to take a shower, review the daily lesson from *A Course in Miracles* and write some of this book. However, before I could get in the shower, my husband wanted to show me something on the computer that he found interesting and thought I'd be interested too. What did I do? I took time out of my schedule to look at the computer, and then I berated myself in the shower for taking too much time, and not saying to my husband, "Thanks, honey. I'd love to look at that later. I need to get in the shower right now so I can be ready for my podcast interview."

How many of you can relate to a scenario like that, where you put someone else's needs or desires first, instead of your own? In years past, I would have stayed angry at myself for an awfully long time and I would have stuffed my feelings with junk food. Then, I would feel even worse!

Today, because of the practices I've done that I've been sharing with you in this book, I stopped beating myself up before I even left the shower! Instead, I forgave myself for not standing up for myself and setting boundaries. I realized that this was a lesson I still needed to learn. I took a breath, and said to myself, "OK. Next time, I'll do better. I'll stop and think before I blindly go along with whatever someone wants me to do. I'll check in with myself and see if this is something I want or need to do right that minute, or I will attempt to get an agreement from the other person to allow me to follow up with them later if it's not convenient for me then."

I'm proud of myself for being able to step back from the brink quickly. I'm a big Billy Joel fan. The lyrics of one of his songs says it all, "You're only human. You're supposed to make mistakes." I'm going to screw up from time to time and slip back into that old familiar people-pleaser mode that I adopted in childhood as a survival mechanism. I encourage you to be kind to yourself as well. Forgive yourself for mistakes you make. Let go of the need to punish yourself. It doesn't do you any good and it doesn't do anyone else any good either. Every time you get down on yourself, it leaves you vulnerable to others who may take advantage of your low self-esteem.

Ultimately, what embracing your divinity means is to love yourself as God loves you. As I've said before, God sends us signs to help us learn these lessons. After I got out of the shower and said down at my desk to review the day's lesson from *A Course in Miracles*, I received another sign. The lesson contained this sentence, "Deep within you is everything that is perfect, ready to radiate through you and out into the whole world." (W-pII. 41.3.1) And then the instruction for the day, was to close my eyes and repeat the day's idea, "God goes with me wherever I go" and then make no effort to think of anything.

When I closed my eyes and repeated that idea to myself, a song lyric popped into my head, "you're gonna turn out fine..." It was from the Andy Grammar song, *Keep Your Head Up*. I googled the lyric after I finished the lesson and laughed out loud at God's message to me. Here are some of the lyrics that stood out to me as being especially appropriate:

I'm seeing all the angles

Thoughts get tangled

I start to compromise

My life and my purpose.

Is it all worth it?

Am I gonna turn out fine?

Oh, you turn out fine.

Fine, oh, you turn out fine.

But you gotta keep your head up, oh,

And you can let your hair down, eh.

You gotta keep your head up, oh,

And you can let your hair down, eh.

I know it's hard, know it's hard,

To remember sometimes,

But you gotta keep your head up, oh,

And you can let your hair down, eh.

LIVE. LOVE. ENGAGE. | 119

I am so grateful that God uses music to communicate with me. That is why I believe it is so important to open your mind and heart to receive messages from your Higher Self. God loves you and wants you to know it. The more you embrace your divinity, trust your instincts, and listen with your heart, the more messages you will see and hear that will provide you with the answers you seek.

Song lyrics are only one way that God communicates with me. Seeing repeating numbers like 333 or 11:11 on a clock are also indications that God, angels, or other spiritual guides are trying to get your attention. During the months I spent writing this book at the beach, I would also get signs from nature. A bird, butterfly, crab would pass by me just when I was struggling over what to write. I would pull out my phone and search the internet for spirit animal meanings, and sure enough, I would find that the creature I had seen had a significant message for me at that moment. One time, I noticed something glittering in the sand, and I bent down and spotted a tiny child's ring with a blue butterfly on it. Butterflies signal transformation, which I was going through in the process of writing this book. And the spiritual meaning of the butterfly is that it is asking you to embrace those changes in your environment and your emotional body. Seeing that butterfly ring and other butterflies since have given me confidence to continue on my spiritual path, which has allowed me to write this book. I give thanks every day for spiritual signs because they draw me closer to God.

CHAPTER 15

ATTITUDE OF GRATITUDE

When I was first given the idea for this book, I knew that God was serious about wanting me to write about love because I received that email from Hay House promoting their Writers' Bootcamp. Included in the book writing course was an opportunity to submit a book proposal for a chance to win a contract to have Hay House publish your book. I procrastinated right up until the deadline to submit the book proposal, before I decided to tackle it. The proposal included writing one complete chapter, as well as chapter summaries and an overview of the book. I spent about two days on the process and submitted the proposal. Needless to say, I did not win. And that was OK because I wasn't ready to write the book then. I needed to learn the lessons I wanted to write about first, as I've shared in earlier chapters.

There was a lot of good that came from that exercise. Much of what I originally wrote made its way into this book. The original outline included a chapter on gratitude. Back then, I thought this concept would be a separate section unto itself - that the letter E in L.O.V.E. also stood for Express Gratitude. But then the acronym would be L.O.V.E.E. and that just didn't look right. LOL! So, what does gratitude have to do with Embracing Your Divinity?

The ultimate act of self-love is to be grateful for YOU, even when you feel unlovable. That simple phrase, "thank you," has as much power to change your life as saying, "I love you."

Thank God for the gift of life you have been given. Thank yourself for taking action to make positive changes in your life, like reading this book. Gratitude is the magic formula to having more love, joy, and abundance in your life.

In fact, being grateful and appreciative for everything you have in your life is your superpower. It can mean the difference between sleepwalking through life, or living a full, rich life that you look forward to waking up to every day. There are so many people who have it rough in this life. There is so much sadness and anger and fear that permeates our waking lives. And yet, if you look around, there is so much beauty to behold. Look outside at the trees, the grass, the blue sky, the clouds. These are nature's bounty, and they serve mankind by giving us the oxygen we need to breathe, the rain to nourish and grow our food, to replenish our lakes and streams and oceans. So much to be thankful for. And we often take it for granted, and do not treat it as kindly as we could.

The more grateful you are for what you have, the more you have to be grateful for. In fact, there is scientific proof of this. A study conducted by psychologists asked a group of participants to record things they were grateful for each week. A second group kept track of things that displeased them, and a third group wrote about events that affected them, with no emphasis on the events being positive or negative. The researchers found that after 10 weeks, the group that focused on gratitude was more optimistic and felt better about their lives. What was even more surprising, is that this group also exercised more and had fewer doctor visits than those who focused on sources of aggravation.

When your life is especially challenging, you may think it's too hard to think of things to be grateful for. I get that. My sister was not happy about getting cancer. But she was grateful for the help she received from me and her friends. If you live in a house or apartment, and you had money to buy this book, that's a lot to be grateful for right there. You're not homeless and penniless.

I want to challenge you to stretch yourself beyond expressing gratitude for the blessings you currently have and be grateful for the things that upset you or make you angry. Here's why. When we experience challenges in our life, it's an opportunity to learn and grow. You've probably heard this saying before: "Why do bad things happen to good people?" For one thing, "bad" is your perception. I know a woman who suffered a terrible tragedy. Both of her sons were killed within a couple of years of each other. One was murdered, and the other died serving his country in Iraq. Those events don't sound like anything to be grateful for, right? I'm positive she's not grateful that they died. However, those events gave her an opportunity to write a series of books about her experiences so that she could help others. That is something for which she can be grateful.

Even though I miss my sister every day, I am grateful for the experience her cancer journey gave me. I had an opportunity to bond with my sister in a unique way. We shared stories about our different childhoods, since there was a ten-year difference in our ages. We got to take a trip to San Diego together so she could see the ocean again. And we baked her favorite Christmas cookies, during which she proceeded to school me on the correct way to flatten the dough. I had to admit she was right; the cookies turned out better. My ego was a bit bruised in the moment, but I am glad she gave me that lesson because I will always remember that day when I bake those cookies in the future.

We had some serious talks too, like what happens after death, and what we believe. And I gained new compassion for those in wheelchairs, as I learned of the challenges in wheeling Michaela around to various stores. (There are still some public restrooms that are not ADA compliant!) I learned about hospice workers and what a tremendous service they provide those facing the end of this earthly life. And of course, the whole experience resulted in this book, for which I am eternally grateful.

We can also be grateful for the people in our life who challenge us. Especially those closest to us. I believe these people are here to shine a light on the things about ourselves that need to be healed. When my daughter was three, I used to say she was three going on thirteen because she acted like a teenager then, always pushing my buttons and testing my limits. I couldn't appreciate it at the time, (because I hadn't done this work), but now I see that she was God's gift to me to heal my low self-esteem. She was able to push my buttons because I didn't have the self-confidence to respond appropriately. Despite this, I am proud to say that my daughter has grown up to be a fearless, brilliant, woman who embraces what makes her feel good; she has chosen her own path. And she has taught me about business, courage, and how to live life fully, on my terms. I must have done something right to have her turn out that well! I'm also blessed to be the parent of an equally good-looking, smart, funny, and kind son who is forging his own path in life, and of whom, I am extremely proud.

L.O.V.E. PRACTICES

Mirror Work

One of the best ways to embrace your divinity is to embrace yourself – to practice self-love. What does that look like? Sure, you can treat yourself to a massage. But I'm suggesting a deeper practice here. Telling yourself that you love YOU! Louise Hay recommended that you look at yourself in the mirror and say to yourself, "(Insert Your Name), I love you." And say it like you really mean it! That's key. She would do that every time she looked in a mirror, even the rearview mirror of the car! I still do this myself. I will stand at the bathroom sink, look right into the mirror, and say, "Gloria, I love you." And it puts a smile on my face. I really do love myself! As one of my coaching clients told me after I suggested it, she felt silly at first, but the more she did it, the better she felt about herself. Try it! You've got nothing to lose and everything to gain.

Ho'oponopono

Another way to embrace your divinity is to take up the Hawaiian practice of Ho'oponopono. (The word translates to correction in English.) I first learned about it from Joe Vitale when I took his Law of Attraction course. Vitale co-wrote a book with Dr. Hew Len called *Zero Limits*, that describes how Dr. Len used this practice to heal a ward of mentally ill criminals at the Hawaii State Hospital. Every day, he would sit in his office, review the files of the prisoners, and say this simple, yet powerful prayer: "I am sorry. Please forgive me. Thank you and I love you." After a few months, patients who were shackled could walk freely, others who were heavily medicated were able to reduce their medications, and those with no chance of being released, were in fact, released and set free.

In interviews, Dr. Len said that at the hospital, he would ask himself, "What is going on in me that I'm experiencing a patient being violent?" And then he would say the prayer for himself. According to Dr. Len, when he sees someone and there is something about that person he does not like, he knows it is a memory of him and he needs to take responsibility for it.

And so it is with us. We create the world we see. Rather than "forgiving someone for wrongs they've done," you can forgive yourself and heal emotional wounds you've suffered in the past by repeating the Ho'oponopono mantra every day. You can use it as a separate meditation or in addition to your daily meditation practice. Sit quietly for a moment, repeat the mantra several times and then ask God for healing and forgiveness.

Gratitude Journal

The power of gratitude can't be overstated, especially as a means to live fully, love deeply and engage authentically. It's practically impossible to be depressed or angry when you start thinking about the blessings you have in your life. I strongly recommend starting a daily journal in which you can keep track of the things, people and events you have to be grateful for. Write at least 3-5 things in this journal every night before you go to bed, or first thing in the morning, or do it both times, whichever feels right for you. The important thing is to just do it!

Meditation

I already recommended meditation at the beginning of the book under the "Let Go and Let God" section, and because I believe it is the most important practice you can undertake, I'm including it again here.

Meditation has been practiced for millennia, with good reason. Practitioners used it as a way to gain insight, wisdom and lasting peace. It's a simple and natural way for you to embrace your divinity. And it provides emotional benefits too including a way to manage your stress, increase your self-awareness, reduce negative emotions while increasing patience and tolerance, and it helps to boost your imagination and increase creativity.

In addition, meditation might offer you some physical benefits too. According to the Mayo Clinic, some research suggests that meditation may help people manage symptoms of conditions such as:

- Anxiety
- Asthma
- Cancer
- Chronic pain
- Depression
- Heart disease
- High blood pressure
- Irritable bowel syndrome
- Sleep problems
- Tension headaches

If you begin a meditation practice with the intention of improving your physical health, that's reason enough to start!

CHAPTER 16

LIVE FULLY, LOVE DEEPLY AND ENGAGE AUTHENTICALLY

The L.O.V.E. Method that God shared with me, and that I have shared with you in the preceding chapters, is an invitation for you to develop a closer relationship with your Higher Self, so you can live fully, love deeply and engage authentically with the world. The four steps: Let Go and Let God, Open Your Heart to Receive, Value Your Uniqueness, and Embrace Your Divinity are intended to guide you on a spiritual journey toward achieving more peace, joy, and abundance in your life. When you incorporate the practices which I have outlined in this book into your life daily, they can help you reduce the self-doubt, confusion, and powerlessness that you may feel, and cultivate more confidence, clarity, and commitment to yourself, so you can shine your light in the world as God intends you to do.

In case you're wondering why I called them "practices" rather than techniques, it's because for best results, you'll always be practicing them. Think of it as strengthening and toning your spiritual muscles. You can't exercise for a few months, stop, and expect to maintain the stamina and muscle strength you gained in the process. After a few months of NOT exercising, your muscles will get flabby, you may gain weight, and you likely won't have as much energy to get up and do the things you enjoy doing each day.

I would like to issue a word of caution here. The road you're about to undertake won't always be easy. In fact, these practices can cause an emotional and even physical upheaval in your life. As an example, one day while writing this book, I endured several hours of severe stomach distress - cramps, diarrhea and nausea. Just as quickly as it came on, the symptoms disappeared, and I felt a compulsion to start writing. This was unlike any writing I had done before. It was a profound spiritual experience - one I'll detail more fully in the future - since new spiritual gifts are awakening in me as I close out this book.

Upheaval happens because you are expanding your spiritual container, and your ego or Isha will want to push back. Realize this is a part of the process - a necessary part. You're also rewiring your neurons and that takes practice, patience, and persistence to accomplish. I wrote a song during the pandemic which illustrates this process and I hope it gives you strength to carry on this work:

> You gotta break down before you break out
> God is here for you
> You gotta break down before you break out
> That's how you break through
>
> Life isn't easy. Life isn't fair.
> Things get confusing when you're not aware
> The answers you seek are right inside you
> Let go and let God, this message is true

You gotta break down before you break out
Love is here for you
You gotta break down before you break out
That's how you break through

You've got power. You've got grace.
Don't be afraid to show your face.
Let your tears fall, and the anger through.
The faster you face it, the better you'll do.

You gotta break down before you break out
God will carry you
You gotta break down before you break out
That's when you break through

So, Shine shine shine
Break out of your shell.
Shine shine shine
The world will know you well
Shine shine shine
This is who you're meant to be
Shine shine shine
The love you see is me

You gotta break down before you break out
God is there with you
You gotta break down before you break out
That's why you break through

Open Your Heart to Receive… Help!

Remember when I talked about my sister exclaiming that getting cancer was a heck of a way to learn how to ask for help? Picking up this book is an excellent first step in getting the help you need to stop doubting yourself and start being yourself. But reading is a solitary endeavor. You don't have to go on this spiritual journey alone. In fact, it's unwise to do so. We are not meant to be solitary creatures. We are social animals, and I believe we are connected spiritually with one another.

Whenever you start a new practice, it's easy to quit without an accountability partner there to cheer you on, lovingly scold you when necessary, or simply be a sounding board for those days when you want to vent. Learning how to truly, madly, and deeply fall in love with yourself is not easy. If it were, the self-help section of Amazon and your local bookstore would be empty!

My advice is to find someone to talk with on a regular basis. It could be a good friend, a coach/counselor, therapist, spiritual guide, or a peer group. If you resonate with me, (and I am guessing you must on some level, otherwise you would not still be reading this book), please reach out to me on my website, GloriaRand.com, and we will explore how we can work together. Always remember that God loves you and wants what is best for you. The Universe has your back. All it takes is a little trust, a little faith and a whole lotta L.O.V.E.

ACKNOWLEDGEMENTS

Writing a book about love was the last thing I could have ever imagined doing in my life, let alone, writing a book about my relationship with God and myself. But here we are. I am grateful to God for making this possible because the writing process has been an emotional journey that has given me the ability to love myself just as I am.

I am grateful for the lessons I've learned from my parents, siblings, husband, and children. They loved me, poked me, and provided a mirror for me to see the limiting beliefs I held about myself.

Thank you to my Wise Woman guide, goddess and friend Patricia Alton, who suggested I go to the beach to write this book, when I was unable to do it at home. Thank you to Milena Cortes Jackson who designed the beautiful heart for the cover of this book. Many thanks to my publisher Michael D. Butler who provided the structure and support to get the book done and in the hands of those who need it most.

Thank you to the coaches, counselors, mentors and authors who inspired me, taught me, and occasionally gave me a loving kick in the butt, including: Jannette Anderson, Diane Shiels Bettencourt, Tasha Chen, Trish Carr, Bo Eason, Jay Fiset, Gerry Foster, Jenn Goddard, AmondaRose Igoe, Robin Quinn Keehn, Harrison Klein,

Elizabeth Gifford Maffei, Nancy Matthews, Michael Patrick Miller, Katheryn Napier, Sherinata Pollock, Tony Robbins, Marty Ward, Rae-ann Wood-Schatz, Rev. Cynthia Alice Anderson, Jennifer Hadley, Jennifer Sigman, Abraham, Deepak Chopra, Alan Cohen, Mike Dooley, Dr. Wayne Dyer, Louise Hay, Esther & Jerry Hicks, the Dalai Lama, Adam Markel, Richard Rohr, Colin Tipping, Eckhart Tolle, Archbishop Desmond Tutu, and Marianne Williamson.

Thank you to my extended family: Jessica Lee Alton, Regina Berman, ML Blanchoff, Brenda Bryan, Rebecca Horne Calvalho, Brad Climer, Crystal-Ra Laksmi Ditton, Michael Ditton, Elena Estanol, Joy Evanns, Marc-Andre Gagnon, Laurie Hock, Tamara L. Hunter, Vicki Ibaugh, Sondra Joyce, Sherry Knight, Rhonda Lowery, Matthew Luckman, Maddox, Michelle McCuller, Diazina Mobley, Lynn Riehl, Lynne Roe, Damien Rufus, Shayn Stevens, Dolores Thomas, James Thomas, Lou Urban, Debb Walker, Daphne Wells, Lee Murphy Wolf, Mark Wolf, and Grace Zimmerman.

Finally, I want to thank my sister Michaela's friends and colleagues who took care of her when I wasn't there, especially Junie Ellen Hostetler and Garnet Roelofson Adair, who continue to shine a light in my life and keep Michaela's memory alive.

ABOUT THE AUTHOR

Known as The Insightful Copywriter, Gloria Grace Rand shares Messages from the Heart as a #1 best-selling Author, Certified High Performance Speaker, host of the Live. Love. Engage. Podcast, and Light Language Channel.

Growing up with an alcoholic father and abusive mother taught Gloria that it was safer to be seen and not heard, so she let music, dance, and writing speak for her. After graduating from Wayne State University with a bachelor's degree in Mass Communications - Radio/TV/Film, Gloria spent nearly two decades in television production, most notably as writer and producer for the award-winning PBS financial news program, "Nightly Business Report." Since launching her company, Web to Wealth Marketing, in 2009, more than 150 companies have hired Gloria to create a profitable online presence for them.

Losing her sister to cancer in 2016 led Gloria on a journey of self-discovery and spiritual awakening, which culminated in the writing of her first book, Live. Love. Engage. Through the divinely inspired practices detailed in the book, she has healed her old emotional wounds. Gloria now shows service-based entrepreneurs how to gain clarity, confidence, and connection to your divine nature, so you can create a business with more Impact, Influence, and Income.

Gloria is a proud member of The Wellness Universe, Women's Prosperity Network, and Women Speakers Association. She is a contributing author to three best-selling books, *Unscripted: How Entrepreneurs Leap and Find Success*, *Conceived to Lead*, and *Connect: 100+ Mind-Blowing Strategies to Use Social Media and Drive Business Growth*. She has been a featured leading expert on Central Florida News 13 TV, has been featured on dozens of podcasts and radio shows, and appeared on national stages with Bill Walsh, Steve Beckles-Ebusua, Madeline Faiella, Paul Finck, Patricia Rogers, Nancy Matthews, Dawn Moore, Roberto Candelaria, Chris Salem, Rey Perez, Mary Jackson, Warren Carlyle, Vishal Morjaria, John Shamburger, Marty L. Ward, Heather, Schooler, Benson Gideon, Harrison Klein, and AmondaRose Igoe.

Gloria believes in contributing her time, talents, and treasure to non-profit organizations. She trained to run marathons and raised money for the American Heart Association and Leukemia & Lymphoma Society. In 2020, she served as Assistant Director for the Tour of Love, a 36-hour livestream fundraising event modeled after the Jerry Lewis MDA Telethon that benefited Chemo Buddies 4Life - CB4L.org. She is honored to be a Peace Ambassador for the Global Peace Challenge 2020, organized, and sponsored under the Peace Abbey, a non-profit founded in 1988 to create, maintain, and promote innovative models for social change that reflect the principles of non-violence that exist within the major faith traditions around the world.

For personal and professional development, including one-on-one transformational coaching, or to book Gloria Grace Rand for a speaking engagement, contact us at www.GloriaRand.com.

Email the author at meetme@gloriarand.com

GLORIA'S RECOMMENDED READING

A Return to Love, Marianne Williamson, HarperCollins Publishers, 1992

A Course in Miracles Made Easy, Alan Cohen, Hay House Inc., 2015

The Power of Now, Eckhart Tolle, New World Library, 1999

The Vortex, Esther and Jerry Hicks, Hay House Inc., 2009

The Tao Made Easy, Alan Cohen, Hay House Inc., 2018

The Universal Christ, Richard Rohr, Convergent Books, 2019

Radical Forgiveness, Colin Tipping, Sounds True, 2009

Grieving Mindfully, Sameet M. Kumar, Ph. D., New Harbinger Publications, 2005

Living, Loving & Learning, Leo F. Buscaglia, Ph. D., Ballantine Books, 1982

Illusions – The Adventures of a Reluctant Messiah, Richard Bach, Delacorte Press, 1977

Infinite Possibilities, Mike Dooley, Atria Books, 2009

Your Erroneous Zones, Wayne W. Dyer, Funk & Wagnalls, 1976

The Brain that Changes Itself, Norman Doidge, M.D., Penguin Group, 2007

Making a Good Brain Great, Daniel G. Amen, M.D., Three Rivers Press, 2005

Hardwiring Happiness, Rick Hanson, Ph.D., Random House, 2013

You Can Heal Your Life, Louise Hay, Hay House Inc., 1984

Jeffrey, K.D. Wagner, MA, Beyond Publishing, 2020

CPSIA information can be obtained
at www.ICGtesting.com
Printed in the USA
LVHW080247300321
682890LV00009B/599